WHY BAD THINGS HAPPEN TO GOOD PEOPLE

BRENT L. TOP

WHY BAD THINGS HAPPEN TO GOOD PEOPLE

Formerly titled *Strength to Endure*

Bookcraft
Salt Lake City, Utah

Library of Congress Catalog Card Number: 90-85479

ISBN 1-57008-321-5

First softcover printing, 1997

Printed in the United States of America

To my parents,
Norman and Alta Top,
whose faithful endurance and good cheer amidst
adversity are an inspiration to me

For verily I say unto you, blessed is he that keepeth my commandments, whether in life or in death; and he that is faithful in tribulation, the reward of the same is greater in the kingdom of heaven.

Ye cannot behold with your natural eyes, for the present time, the design of your God concerning those things which shall come hereafter, and the glory which shall follow after much tribulation.

For after much tribulation come the blessings. Wherefore the day cometh that ye shall be crowned with much glory; the hour is not yet, but is nigh at hand.

—D&C 58:2–4

Contents

Preface

Adversity and affliction, to greater or lesser degree, are universal conditions of the human experience. None can completely escape the sorrows and sufferings of the second estate. It has been so since Adam and Eve entered the lone and dreary world and will continue until the end of time. Tribulation is not only a universal mortal experience but also an essential element in the plan of salvation. "For it must needs be," Lehi taught his son Jacob, "that there is an opposition in all things" (2 Nephi 2:11). In this dispensation the Lord has affirmed that "if they never should have bitter they could not know the sweet" (D&C 29:39). Finding sweetness amidst bitterness is one of the most difficult challenges of mortality, especially if we feel that by virtue of our righteous living and our gospel understanding we should be spared such suffering and sorrow. Gospel principles, understood and practiced, cannot completely *isolate* us from hardship and heartaches, but they can and do *insulate* us. Bruce C. Hafen insightfully observed:

> Emphasizing God's mercy may lead some to believe they are entitled to divine protection against all of life's natural adversities. There is already enough theological difficulty for those who believe that their activity in the Church should somehow protect them from tragedy and sorrow. Our understanding of the Atonement is hardly a shield against sorrow; rather, it is a rich source of strength to deal productively with the disappointments and heart-breaks that form the deliberate fabric of mortal life. The gospel was given us to heal our pain, not to prevent it. (*The Broken Heart*, p. 5.)

It is the intent of this book to teach those healing gospel principles in such a way that the reader may find some substantive answers to the universal *why* question, Why is this happening to me? Additionally, I hope that this book will provide a "rich source of strength" by addressing a more significant question—the universal *what* question, What can I do to find comfort and consolation? This book does not pretend to possess all the answers for life's difficult questions or the solutions for all suffering and sorrow, but perhaps it can help bring increased perspective and peace. Increased perspective can come as we more fully understand the answers to those universal questions, but peace and solace come only as spiritual gifts from God.

As a result of experiencing my own personal trials and observing family and friends as they deal with adversity, I have asked many questions, pondered much, and sought answers and understanding. I have garnered much from the thoughtful ideas and experiences of others, including great writers and thinkers and humble, faithful Saints. I have added some of my own personal musings and a smattering of my personal studies in the school of adversity. However, the sacred scriptures and the teachings of the prophets comprise the foundation and framework of my writing. I have a strong love for the Brethren and a deep respect for their priesthood positions and the accompanying mantle of authority. I believe they are empowered and inspired to instruct us by virtue of their greater vision of the vast eternal vistas which lie before us. They have a holy mandate to lead, counsel, and comfort the membership of the Church, and thus what they say is what the Lord would have us know and understand on this subject.

My personal quest to better understand the causes and purposes of adversity has helped me to find greater peace and purpose. I hope that the thoughts presented here will likewise help others "deal productively with the disappointments and heartbreaks that form the deliberate fabric of mortal life" and come unto Christ and partake of the peace and comfort that he alone can give.

I wish to express appreciation to hundreds of former students and other people I have associated with through the years as I have presented in classes and lectures the ideas contained in this book. Invariably I came away from such discussions having learned more than I taught. I have been instructed and inspired by the examples and insights of many who have suffered much more than I. As a result of their faithful endurance they often are able to know and understand more than I could ever teach them. To them and to all who patiently endure life's many adversities and who serve so well despite sorrow and suffering, I express my admiration and appreciation and pay tribute with this book.

CHAPTER ONE

More Questions Than Answers

Why do bad things happen to good people? Why would a loving, merciful Father in Heaven allow his children to suffer all manner of tragedies, trials, and tribulations? Why would he create a world seemingly designed for the happiness of man yet enveloped in crime and corruption, pain and poverty, and sin and suffering? Such questions are not new. Great philosophers and theologians of all ages have wrestled with the apparent contradictions between the theology of a God of perfect love and beneficence and the reality of a world of injustices, inequities, and misery. Such contradictions often defy the best logic of both philosopher and theologian.

Why does God tolerate a world where a drunken driver can crash into an oncoming car, snuffing out the lives of a young family and, more often than not, walking away from the accident unhurt and sometimes even unaccountable?

Why do some survive in plane crashes and others die? Do not the passengers who die exercise faith in God and plead for preservation just as much as, or perhaps even more than, those who are spared?

Why does a young father suffer an untimely death, leaving a widow and several small children to mourn his loss? Why must they be left alone to face an uncertain financial future?

Why do missionaries sometimes die in the mission field? Why are they not protected and preserved, especially when they are anxiously engaged in the service of the Lord?

Why does God permit the kidnapping, exploitation, and murder of innocent children? What good could possibly come from such outrageous suffering?

Why does he allow criminals to prosper in their crimes? Why does it often seem that the wicked become wealthy as they mockingly break both civil and natural laws? How can he allow the drug dealer to indulge himself with a life of luxury at the expense of the drug abuser who is a slave in the squalor of the streets?

Why are some miraculously healed of terrible illnesses and yet others who may be more worthy and faithful are left to suffer and die? Why must the miseries of mortality force some to suffer excruciating pain for periods that extend beyond days and weeks into months and years? Why does God seem to ignore cries of anguish from those who must often stand helplessly by, witnessing the deterioration of a dear one while his agony seems needlessly prolonged?

Why are so many parents' hearts broken by the apostasy or alienation of their children? How can God countenance the crushing of the hearts of faithful, loving husbands and wives by the thoughtless infidelity of selfish spouses? How can he allow the abuse of wives and children? Why are so many innocent children's lives shattered by divorce or deprivation?

Why must some face so many trials and tribulations in mortality, while others "breeze" through life seemingly untouched by suffering and sorrow?

Why does God intervene some times but not others? Why did he lengthen the life of King Hezekiah of Judah, one individual (see Isaiah 38:1-9; 2 Kings 20:1-7), yet allow the myriad unconscionable horrors of the Holocaust, wherein millions suffered and died?

When such concerns and questions are raised, we are often inclined to feel that the restored gospel of Jesus Christ has all of the right answers for all of the hard questions. Surely the gospel does have many of the answers in the religious context. A study of the scriptures and the teachings of latter-day prophets gives us glimpses of understanding but also painfully reminds us that there are often more questions than answers and that some explanations must simply wait.

A few years ago I saw this principle profoundly demonstrated in a religion class as the students were responding to many of the difficult questions previously mentioned. There was much discussion among them. I was impressed with their logic and their knowledge of the scriptures. Virtually all of the students made comments that reflected their confidence that the gospel has the answers to the problem of pain in the world. With every situation I presented, a student had a gospel answer for, or a theological reconciliation of, the apparent inequities of life. After much discussion, however, one student raised his hand to speak. He was older than most of the students in the class.

He had also been noticeably quiet during our theological discussion. His voice cracking with emotion, he taught us all a lesson about questions and answers.

"The things you have been saying are right," he said, choking back the tears. "I have been taught those things from my youth. I have searched the scriptures, served a mission, and been active in the Church all my life. I have a testimony of the truthfulness of the gospel, and I have an understanding of the role of adversity in the plan of salvation, but . . ." At this point the tears flowed both from his eyes and ours. Haltingly he continued, "But it didn't make it easier to gather my three children around me and tell them that their mommy had just died. Even though I too know many of the answers to life's difficult questions, I am still lonely, and I ask over and over again, *Why?* Why did she have to die? Why am I left alone?" As he spoke, the students were experiencing feelings that most of them had never had before. They were learning about unanswerable questions and unconsoling answers they had never faced before. "You have the answers," he told his fellow students. "But have you ever had to ask the questions?" As the bell rang ending the class period, sobered students, who had been so full of gospel answers before and during class, now filed out with more questions than answers.

It is not uncommon for us to feel guilty for questioning in times of adversity. Sometimes we may erroneously view questioning God's wisdom and his purposes for our suffering and heartaches as a departure from the faith or a wavering of our commitment to the gospel. There is comfort, however, in recognizing that those with the most insight and inspiration as to God's will for mankind are often the ones who do the most poignant pleading and questioning.

The prophet Jeremiah, who had suffered much personally and witnessed much tribulation among his people, searchingly questioned the Lord: "Righteous art thou, O Lord, when I plead with thee: yet let me talk with thee of thy judgments: Wherefore doth the way of the wicked prosper? wherefore are all they happy that deal very treacherously? . . . How long shall the land mourn, and the herbs of every field wither, for the wickedness of them that dwell therein?" (Jeremiah 12:1, 4.) Even Jeremiah, with his prophetic mantle and understanding, questioned the Lord in his anguish. Despite his testimony and faith, there were some questions he could not answer.

Perhaps the most famous of sufferers in the scriptures was Job. The Lord described Job as "a perfect and an upright man, one that feareth God, and escheweth evil" (Job 2:3). He lost home and financial security; he suffered the deaths of his children; he was cursed and ridiculed by friends and loved ones; and he was afflicted with painful physical maladies. "In all this Job sinned not, nor charged God foolishly" (Job 1:22). He was a model of faith, integrity, endurance, and patience in affliction. Yet this man, who had declared "Though he slay me, yet will I trust in him" (Job 13:15), also found that he had more distressing questions than comfortable answers. In his anguish he questioned: "Why died I not from the womb? why did I not give up the ghost when I came out of the belly?" (Job 3:11.) "My soul is weary of my life; I will leave my complaint upon myself; I will speak in the bitterness of my soul. I will say unto God, Do not condemn me; shew me wherefore thou contendest with me. Is it good unto thee that thou shouldest oppress, that thou shouldest despise the work of thine hands, and shine upon the counsel of the wicked?" (Job 10:1–3.) In addition Job asked the ancient question that lingers still, Why must one who is righteous and strives to serve the Lord suffer so much affliction in life? Though his faith was perfect and his testimony of the Redeemer sure, Job struggled with his own questions. It was as his friends ignorantly and unfairly chided him:

"Behold, thou hast instructed many, and thou hast strengthened the weak hands. Thy words have upholden him that was falling, and thou hast strengthened the feeble knees. But now it is come upon thee, and thou faintest; it toucheth thee, and thou art troubled." (Job 4:3–5.)

The great Book of Mormon prophet Alma provided many doctrinal answers concerning the purposes of suffering in mortality. He taught much concerning both the justice and mercy of God in relationship to man's mortal miseries. Despite his doctrinal insight and sure testimony, he too had questions. When he and Amulek were imprisoned in Ammonihah, they were bound with cords and forced to witness the horrifying sight of innocent women and children being burned alive. Unable to intervene, they were left to gaze upon the grisly scene and hear the terrible cries of agony. In addition to watching others suffer, they were beaten, mocked, starved, and persecuted beyond description themselves. In despair Alma cried, "How long shall we suffer these great afflictions, O Lord?" (Alma 14:26.)

Echoing the doleful cries of Alma and Amulek are the earnest queries of a latter-day prophet—the head of this dispensation—the Prophet Joseph Smith. The Prophet's own suffering in the inhumane conditions of Liberty Jail was heightened as he heard of the plunderings, murders, and rapes of the Saints as they were driven from their homes under the infamous "extermination order." Although Joseph had gazed upon the expanses of eternity, had received countless revelations, and had communed with and been taught by glorious beings from the Eternal Presence, in the agony of his own suffering he had more questions than answers. "O God, where art thou? And where is the pavilion that covereth thy hiding place? How long shall thy hand be stayed, and thine eye, yea thy pure eye, behold from the eternal heavens the wrongs of thy people and of thy servants, and thine ear be penetrated with their cries? Yea, O Lord, how long shall they suffer these wrongs and unlawful oppressions, before thine heart shall be softened toward them, and thy bowels be moved with compassion toward them?'' (D&C 121:1–3.)

Not only have prophets through the ages entreated the Lord concerning the seeming injustices of life; even the Savior, when faced with the incomprehensible agonies of Gethsemane and Golgotha, asked, ''My God, my God, why hast thou forsaken me?'' (Matthew 27:46.) His divine nature knew the asnwers, yet his mortal nature questioned, when he was confronted with a suffering that surprisingly surpassed even his own understanding and expectations. Elder Neal A. Maxwell declared:

> Imagine, Jehovah, the Creator of this and other worlds, ''astonished''! Jesus knew cognitively what he must do, but not experientially. He had never personally known the exquisite and exacting process of an atonement before. Thus, when the agony came in its fulness, it was so much, much worse than even He with his unique intellect had ever imagined! No wonder an angel appeared to strengthen him (see Luke 22:43)!
>
> The cumulative weight of all mortal sins—past, present, and future—pressed upon that perfect, sinless, and sensivite Soul! All our infirmities and sicknesses were somehow, too, a part of the awful arithmetic of the Atonement. (See Alma 7:11–12; Isaiah 53:3–5; Matthew 8:17.) The anguished Jesus not only pled with the Father that the hour and cup might pass from Him, but with this relevant citation. ''And he said, Abba, Father, all things are possible unto thee; take away this cup from me'' (Mark 14:35–36). . . .
>
> In this extremity, did He, perchance, hope for a rescuing ram in the thicket? I do not know. His suffering—as it were, *enormity* multiplied by *infinity*—evoked His later

soul-cry on the cross, and it was a cry of forsakenness (see Matthew 27:46). (" 'Willing to Submit,' " pp. 72–73.)

Modern prophets likewise are not exempt from the trials of tribulation; nor are they nonattenders of the school of suffering and sorrow. Therefore, they are often most qualified in their ministry to succor and strengthen others who suffer. Two such prophets, President Harold B. Lee and President Spencer W. Kimball, suffered extraordinary adversity in their own lives but also soothed—by sermon and service—other hearts aching with hardships. Despite their incredible ability to comfort and strengthen others and their abiding faith and testimonies, they also knew that often it is beyond our ability to fully understand the Lord's purposes for our tribulations. In their own moments of distress they too were left to ask unanswerable questions. Elder Spencer W. Kimball's classic address "Tragedy or Destiny?" acknowledges the perplexity of these painfully persistent queries which are part and parcel with mortality.

The daily newspaper screamed the headlines: "Plane Crash Kills 43. No Survivors of Mountain Tragedy," and thousands of voices joined in a chorus: "Why did the Lord let this terrible thing happen?"

Two automobiles crashed when one went through a red light, and six people were killed. Why would God not prevent this?

Why should the young mother die of cancer and leave her eight children motherless? Why did not the Lord heal her?

A little child was drowned; another was run over. Why?

A man died one day suddenly of a coronary occlusion as he climbed a stairway. His body was found slumped on the floor. His wife cried out in agony, "Why? Why would the Lord do this to me? Could he not have considered my three little children who still need a father?"

A young man died in the mission field and people critically questioned: "Why did not the Lord protect this youth while he was doing proselyting work?"

I wish I could answer these questions with authority, but I cannot. I am sure that sometime we'll understand and be reconciled. But for the present we must seek understanding as best we can in the gospel principles. . . .

Did the Lord cause the man to suffer a heart attack? Was the death of the missionary untimely? Answer, if you can. I cannot, for though I know God has a major role in our lives, I do not know how much he causes to happen and how much he merely permits. Whatever the answer to this question, there is another I feel sure about.

Could the Lord have prevented these tragedies? The answer is, Yes. The Lord is omnipotent, with all power to control our lives, save us pain, prevent all accidents, drive all planes and cars, feed us, protect us, save us from labor, effort, sickness, even from death, if he will. But he will not. (In *Faith Precedes the Miracle,* pp. 95–96.)

As we face our own unique Gethsemanes and Golgothas each of us will undoubtedly question the Lord's purposes and gropingly implore, as the Savior did, "Father, Father, why has thou forsaken me?" We will all face the uncomfortable realization that for now, here in mortality, there are more questions than answers. Furthermore, with our finite minds, we would probably not understand, or perhaps not even like, the answers if they were given to us. For as the Lord reminds us: "My thoughts are not your thoughts, neither are your ways my ways. . . . For as the heavens are higher than the earth, so are my ways higher than your ways, and my thoughts than your thoughts." (Isaiah 55:8–9.)

We are not left, however, in total ignorance. Our merciful Father has provided us with holy scriptures and modern revelations which lend eternal perspective and guidance to our limited mortal understanding. Though we still "see through a glass darkly," as Paul said, the truths of the restored gospel can enlighten our path and guide our footsteps, even when we may not be completely consoled and our questions still linger. Such gospel perspective supremely surpasses that perspective acquired only through logic and learning. "The ultimate human questions are really 'why' questions!" said Elder Neal A. Maxwell. "The gospel is positively 'brim' with answers to the 'why' queries concerning human purpose. Gospel truths are the vital integrating and ordering truths, not only telling us of 'things as they really are' but also 'as they really will be' (Jacob 4:13)." (" 'Yet Thou Art There,' " p. 31.)

Celestial character development begins with finding true answers through sincere, soul-searching questions. Yet while we may have many answers in the gospel, those answers may not impact the soul profoundly or permanently until our own experiences impel us to ask the hard questions of life. Those who have arrived at gospel answers to life's difficult dilemmas merely by study may not come to that higher level of understanding that comes only to those who "study" in the school of suffering and sorrow. In this unique educational experience the questions become more important than mere answers—the feelings more instructive than simple facts. When coupled with serious study of the scriptures and conformity to the counsel of living prophets, these questions forged in the crucible of adversity are an integral part of the developmental *process*. This process prepares us to receive the *product*—comfort, consolation, and comprehension. This promised peace and ultimate understanding flow from the Savior as spiritual gifts *after* we have struggled with this process and have eaten "the bread of adversity" and drunk "the water of affliction" (see Isaiah 30:20). The true source of comfort and comprehension is not in the answers, but in him who invites us, "Come unto me, all ye that labour and are heavy laden, and I will give you rest. Take my yoke upon you, and learn of me; for I am meek and lowly in heart: and ye shall find rest unto your souls." (Matthew 11:28–29.) Elder Neal A. Maxwell stated:

> To those of you who so suffer and who, nevertheless, so endure and so testify by the eloquence of your examples, we salute you in Christ! Please forgive those of us who clumsily try to comfort you. We know from whence your true comfort comes. God's "bosom" is there to be leaned upon.
>
> Jesus' promised peace is a special form of rest amid unrest. . . .
>
> We can confidently cast our cares upon the Lord because, through the agonizing events of Gethsemane and Calvary, atoning Jesus is already familiar with our sins, sicknesses, and sorrows (see 1 Peter 5:7; 2 Nephi 9:21; Alma 7:11–12). He can carry them now because He has successfully carried them before (see 2 Nephi 9:8)! (" 'Yet Thou Art There,' " pp. 32–33.)

It is not the objective of this book to give simple or trite answers to life's most difficult and complex questions. Consolation comes not from "self-help" books but only from the Comforter. It is my hope, however, that the principles that are discussed in this book will stimulate searching—of the standard works and of one's soul. I cannot give answers, but I offer instead insights that may contribute to the mortal learning process. Each of us individually must yield to that process if we desire to find comfort, understanding, and that "peace of God, which passeth all understanding, [which] shall keep [our] hearts and minds through Christ Jesus" (Philippians 4:7).

CHAPTER TWO

Why "Bad Things" Happen to Good People

While it is true that we may not be able to discern fully the reasons for suffering and adversity in *specific* cases, we can observe principles and teachings that may provide *general* answers. Despite being handicapped by a finite view of God's dealings with his children, we must, as Elder Spencer W. Kimball admonished, "seek understanding as best we can in the gospel principles" (*Faith Precedes the Miracle*, p. 96). The scriptures and the inspired teachings of the Lord's anointed servants, as well as the insights and experiences of others who have partaken of the "bread of adversity," will not only give us valuable perspective and understanding but also remind us that we are not forsaken or alone in our anguish. Why do "bad things" happen to good people? Why is mortal life so full of ironies and inequities, sorrow and suffering, agony and adversity? In response to these and many other similar queries, the scriptures illuminate three basic causes of suffering: agency, natural law, and the works of God.

Agency

One of the fundamental laws of heaven is the principle of agency, or in other words the power to choose, to exercise one's own will. Lehi taught that "the Lord God gave unto man that he should act for himself" (2 Nephi 2:16). Later in the same discourse, he further declared: "Wherefore, men are free according to the flesh; and all things are given them which are expedient unto man. And they are free to choose liberty and eternal life, through the great Mediator of all men, or to choose captivity and death, according to the captivity and power of the devil; for he seeketh that all men might be miserable like unto himself." (2 Nephi 2:27.)

Numerous other scriptural passages testify of the eternal impact of being able to choose for ourselves. Jacob urged his people to "remember that ye are free to act for yourselves—to choose the way of everlasting death or the way of eternal life" (2 Nephi 10:23). From the walls of Zarahemla, Samuel, the Lamanite prophet, likewise testified:

> And now remember, remember, my brethren, that whosoever perisheth, perisheth unto himself; and whosoever doeth iniquity, doeth it unto himself; for behold, ye are free; ye are permitted to act for yourselves; for behold, God hath given unto you a knowledge and he hath made you free.
>
> He hath given unto you that ye might know good from evil, and he hath given unto you that ye might choose life or death; and ye can do good and be restored unto that

which is good, or have that which is good restored unto you; or ye can do evil, and have that which is evil restored unto you. (Helaman 14:30–31.)

The power to choose is an unfettered gift of God. "Free independence of mind which heaven has so graciously bestowed upon the human family," stated the Prophet Joseph Smith, "[is] one of its choicest gifts" (*Teachings of the Prophet Joseph Smith,* p. 49). Agency is a fundamental principle of the gospel that is essential to man's salvation. There can be no exaltation without agency. President David O. McKay testified of the paramount importance of agency in God's plan of salvation:

> Next to the bestowal of life itself, the right to direct our lives is God's greatest gift to man. Freedom of choice is more to be treasured than any possession earth can give. It is inherent in the spirit of man. It is a divine gift to every normal being. . . . It is the impelling source of the soul's progress. It is the purpose of the Lord that man become like him. In order for man to achieve this, it was necessary for the Creator first to make him free. . . . Without this divine power to choose, humanity cannot progress. ("Man's Free Agency—an Eternal Principle of Progress," p. 1073.)

Because of this supreme significance, agency is a protected principle. "Because *free agency* is a God-given precondition to the purpose of mortal life," wrote Elder Dallin H. Oaks, "no person or organization can take away our free agency in mortality" ("Free Agency and Freedom," p. 9). In order to safeguard the purposes of this mortal probation the Lord will not infringe upon the free exercise of agency. While this promotes the progression of humanity, it also carries with it certain "side effects" that may bring about suffering and sorrow. Agency is linked to adversity in that many times our ordeals and ailments result from the use and/or misuse of agency. Sometimes our woes and worries are direct consequences of the exercise of the power of choice by ourselves or others. "How could we learn about obedience," asked Elder Neal A. Maxwell, "if we were shielded from the consequences of our disobedience?" ("Patience," p. 220.)

Suffering as a Consequence
of the Actions of Others

Each day we are surrounded by suffering and pain resulting from actions and misuse of agency on the part of others. The newspaper headlines and articles almost daily abound in accounts of murder, rape, robbery, and countless other injustices. Through the graphic visual images of television we are continually reminded of the crime and corruption that inflict so much suffering on humanity. The fact that all too often the innocent must suffer at the hands of the wicked seems to be the ultimate irony and inequity of life. Why does God allow the wicked and corrupt of the world to persecute and victimize the righteous and devout, the innocent and helpless? No doubt the unsettling answer lies in the fact that agency is a guarded and treasured principle. As a result, all manner of choices must be tolerated. This, in turn, may inflict inconvenience, misfortune, and hardship to a heinous degree into the lives of others.

C. S. Lewis described this phenomenon in this way: "The possibility of pain is inherent in the very existence of a world where souls can meet. When souls become wicked they will certainly use this possibility to hurt one another; and this, perhaps, accounts for four-fifths of the sufferings of men. It is men, not God, who have produced racks, whips, prisons, slavery, guns, bayonets, and bombs; it is by human avarice or human stupidity, not by the churlishness of nature, that we have poverty and over-work." (*The Problem of Pain*, p. 89.)

Some proclaim, however, that God is cruel for allowing such atrocities. Sometimes we want to blame him, when in truth *he* is surely more sorrowful over such misuse and abuse of his gift of agency than even *we* are. Indeed, as he lamented the wickedness of his children, the Lord actually wept in the presence of his prophet Enoch. Astonished by this, Enoch asked, "How is it that thou canst weep, seeing thou art holy, and from all eternity to all eternity?" (Moses 7:28-29.) The Lord explained:

> Behold these thy brethren; they are the workmanship of mine own hands, and I gave unto them their knowledge, in the day I created them; and in the Garden of Eden, gave I unto man his agency;
>
> And unto thy brethren have I said, and also given commandment, that they should love one another, and that they should choose me, their Father; but behold, they are without affection, and they hate their own blood. . . .
>
> . . . wherefore should not the heavens weep, seeing these shall suffer? (Moses 7:32-33, 37.)

Perhaps the scriptural episode that best exemplifies the concepts involved here is the previously mentioned account of Alma and Amulek at Ammonihah. Imprisoned for preaching to the hardened and wicked inhabitants at Ammonihah, they were subjected to a most "cruel and unusual punishment." In addition to having to bear their own suffering and deprivations they were brought forth and compelled to witness the massive slaughter of innocent women and children—loved ones of men who had been persecuted and driven out for accepting the teachings of Alma. One can hardly imagine the terrible sights and sounds of innocent women and children being burned alive as a punishment for believing the words of God. Why would God allow such unjust and torturous treatment of his righteous Saints? The scriptural account helps us to better understand God's dealings in this and other similarly difficult dilemmas.

> And when Amulek saw the pains of the women and children who were consuming in the fire, he also was pained; and he said unto Alma: How can we witness this awful scene? Therefore let us stretch forth our hands, and exercise the power of God which is in us, and save them from the flames.
>
> But Alma said unto him: The Spirit constraineth me that I must not stretch forth mine hand; for behold the Lord receiveth them up unto himself in glory; *and he doth suffer that they may do this thing, or that the people may do this thing unto them, according to the hardness of their hearts,* that the judgments which he shall exercise upon them in his wrath may be just; and the blood of the innocent shall stand as a witness against them, yea, and cry mightily against them at the last day. (Alma 14:10–11, italics added.)

Because he protects the principle of agency, the Lord "suffered," or allowed, the wicked citizens of Ammonihah to inflict great suffering upon two chosen prophets and to put innocent and faithful Saints to death. To do otherwise, even in such a noble cause, would smack of Lucifer's premortal efforts to "destroy the agency of man" (Moses 4:3). There will be painful consequences as a result of man's free exercise of agency, but the Lord in his loving kindness also has promised compassionate compensation. This type of divine compensation is seen in Captain Moroni's epistle to Pahoran: "For the Lord suffereth the righteous to be slain that his justice and judgment may come upon the wicked; therefore ye need not suppose that the righteous are lost because they are slain; but behold, they do enter into the rest of the Lord their God" (Alma 60:13).

Suffering as a result of the misuse of agency on the part of others was also prevalent in the early history of the Church in this dispensation. The Saints that had settled in Jackson County were faced with enormous opposition and persecution at the hands of Missouri ruffians. The Church's printing press had been destroyed, Saints had been beaten and tarred and feathered, faithful members were being expelled from their homes while judges and civic leaders repeatedly refused to administer justice or offer relief. The Prophet Joseph was instructed of the Lord to organize a body of men whose mission would be to "redeem the land" and assist the suffering Saints and return them to their homes. In the course of the revelation the Lord again revealed his purposes in allowing such a vexation to come upon his people.

> Verily I say unto you, my friends, behold, I will give unto you a revelation and commandment, that you may know how to act in the discharge of your duties concerning the salvation and redemption of your brethren, who have been scattered on the land of Zion;
> Being driven and smitten by the hands of mine enemies, on whom I will pour out my wrath without measure in mine own time.
> For I have suffered them thus far, that they might fill up the measure of their iniquities, that their cup might be full. (D&C 103:1–3.)

It is clear from this revelation that—because the wicked are accountable for their actions, and their misuse of agency will ultimately bring their own condemnation—the Lord "suffer[s] them" to persecute and torment the righteous. "I the Lord search the heart, I try the reins, even to give every man according to . . . the fruit of his doings" (Jeremiah 17:10). If the Lord were to interfere with every negative action of man not only would he violate our sacred agency, but also the law of the harvest would be negated. We could not "reap" if we were not allowed to "sow" (see Galatians 6:7–8). "All through the ages some of the righteous have had to suffer," declared President Joseph Fielding Smith, "because of the acts of the unrighteous, but they will get their reward" (*Doctrines of Salvation* 3:37).

Elder Spencer W. Kimball further explained: "The basic gospel law is free agency and eternal development. To force us to be careful or righteous would be to nullify that fundamental law and make growth impossible. . . . If all the sick for whom we pray were healed, if all the righteous were protected and the wicked destroyed, the whole program of the Father would be annulled and the basic principle of the gospel, free agency, would be ended. No man would have to live by faith." (*Faith Precedes the Miracle*, pp. 96–97.)

An earlier prophet, Mormon, speaking of the death, destruction, suffering, and tribulations caused by the Nephite-Lamanite wars, illustrated the two extreme results of the use of agency and explained that much of the apparent inequality in life comes as a result of sin.

> And from the first year to the fifteenth has brought to pass the destruction of many thousand lives; yea, it has brought to pass an awful scene of bloodshed.
>
> And the bodies of many thousands are laid low in the earth, while the bodies of many thousands are moldering in heaps upon the face of the earth; yea, and many thousands are mourning for the loss of their kindred, because they have reason to fear, according to the promises of the Lord, that they are consigned to a state of endless wo.
>
> While many thousands of others truly mourn for the loss of their kindred, yet they rejoice and exult in the hope, and even know, according to the promises of the Lord, that they are raised to dwell at the right hand of God, in a state of never-ending happiness.

And thus we see how great the inequailty of man is because of sin and transgression, and the power of the devil,
which comes by the cunning plans which he hath devised
to ensnare the hearts of men. (Alma 28:10-13.)

While we often suffer because of the sins of others, we
must remember that transgression and misuse of agency,
as sources of suffering, are two directional—they may be
externally inflicted, or they may be self-inflicted. We may
cause some of our own misery.

Suffering as a Consequence
of Our Own Actions

In the revelation regarding the suffering and persecution of the Saints in Missouri, the Lord not only con-
demned the mobocrats but also put blame on some of the
members of the Church. He said that he had suffered his
enemies "thus far, that they might fill up the measure of
their iniquities, that their cup might be full; and that those
who call themselves after my name might be chastened for
a little season with a sore and grievous chastisement, because they [the Saints] did not hearken altogether unto the
precepts and commandments which I gave unto them"
(D&C 103:3-4).

Clearly the Lord showed these early Latter-day Saints
that their afflictions not only resulted from the wicked actions of their enemies and oppressors but also stemmed
from the "jarrings, and contentions, and envyings, and
strifes, and lustful and covetous desires among them"
(D&C 101:6). Moreover, some of the Saints foolishly provoked the lawless frontiersmen with vain and boastful actions. In corresponding with leaders of the Church in
Missouri regarding the plight of the Saints there the
Prophet Joseph Smith declared, "This affliction is sent
upon us not for your sins, but for the sins of the Church"

(in Lyndon W. Cook, *The Revelations of the Prophet Joseph Smith*, p. 205).

Examples of self-inflicted suffering resulting from personal sins and individual actions are as common as news reports of the crimes and atrocities that are perpetrated by the wicked and careless upon the faithful and careful. Elder Boyd K. Packer has observed that "often, very often, we are punished as much *by* our sins as we are *for* them" (*Teach Ye Diligently*, p. 262, italics added). This principle is graphically reflected in the Book of Mormon account of Zeezrom. After contending against the preaching of Alma and Amulek and seeing these prophets and those who believed their words persecuted and imprisoned, Zeezrom became sick with, as the scriptures record, "a burning fever, which was caused by the great tribulations of his mind on account of his wickedness" (Alma 15:3). Our own foolishness and sinfulness can produce suffering and tribulation similar to that of Zeezrom. This suffering may manifest itself in two ways—painful problems resulting from our own recalcitrance and loss of blessings and peace that could have been ours in righteousness. In connection with this eternal law of justice (see Alma 41:10; D&C 130:20–21), the following excerpts from the writings of Elder Joseph Fielding Smith provide some helpful insights:

> Are we serving the Lord? Are we keeping his commandments? Or are we following the trend of the times and the evils of the times? . . . The troubles we see on every side are the result of wickedness. They do not come from righteousness. These things do not come because the people are loving the Lord, but because they have forsaken him.
>
> It is because men violate the commandments of God and refuse to hearken unto his word; and these things are in

fulfilment of the predictions that have been made by the prophets of old and also the prophets in our own time. . . .

It is not the will of the Lord that there should come upon the people disaster, trouble, calamity, and depression (as we have got into the habit of speaking of some of our troubles), but because man himself will violate the commandments of God and will not walk in righteousness, the Lord permits all of these evils to come upon him. In the beginning, the Lord blessed the earth for men's sake. It was his intention that men, if they would only keep the commandments of the Lord, should have the good things of the earth and live in peace and happiness in the spirit of righteousness. . . .

. . . But, men are rebellious; they are not willing to live in that law and profit thereby; they are not willing to receive the good things of the earth as the Lord would give to them in abundance; but in their narrow-mindedness, shortsightedness, and in their greed and selfishness, they think they know better than the Lord does. And so, they pursue another course, and the result is that the blessings of the Lord are withdrawn, and in the place thereof come calamity, destruction, plagues, and violence. Men have themselves to blame.

We sometimes wonder why we have affliction. We wonder why we do not have the best of health. From this which I have read [D&C 93:40–43], we may very properly infer that affliction sometimes comes upon us because we ourselves are not faithful in the performance of duty and in keeping the commandments of the Lord.

What a pity it is that people will pay little heed to sacred counsels, and in their madness and love of the things of the world take the hard road and have to receive punishment when there is a means of escape. When these calamities come, what right have the people of Zion to expect protection! (*Doctrines of Salvation* 3:26–29.)

As Elder Smith pointed out, our own prideful pursuits, foolishness, and greediness may bring upon us suffering much the same as that brought by blatant wickedness or rebellion. This is because we often are stubbornly determined to do what we want to do, not what *God* wants us to do. When we do this we not only reap the consequences of our actions but also further exacerbate our predicament through cutting ourselves off from the protecting, guiding influence of the Holy Spirit. King Benjamin declared: "And now, I say unto you, my brethren, that after ye have known and have been taught all these things, if ye should transgress and go contrary to that which has been spoken, that ye do withdraw yourselves from the Spirit of the Lord, that it may have no place in you to guide you in wisdom's paths that ye may be blessed, prospered, and preserved" (Mosiah 2:36).

When, through the misuse of agency, we "withdraw" ourselves from the Spirit it is understandable how suffering and setbacks can result. Financial difficulties that bring enormous tribulation and emotional distress often come as a result of foolishness, greed, or disregard of the inspired words of the prophets. A drug addict whose life is one of physical torment and who is subjected to the squalor and violence of the streets has brought at least some of his own suffering upon himself. An adulterer who destroys a marriage and family must recognize not only that he has inflicted pain upon the lives of others but also that he must experience the consequential side effects of his sin on himself. Sometimes even health problems and the accompanying physical and emotional distresses come as a result of our own unwise choices. For example, a person who acquires a deadly disease through immoral or other sinful behavior cannot claim that he is an "innocent victim." Rabbi Harold S. Kushner, author of *When Bad*

Things Happen to Good People, in that book provides this insightful observation:

> As we have learned more about how the human body works, as we understand more of the natural laws built in to the world, we have some answers. We have come to understand that we cannot indefinitely abuse our bodies and neglect our health without increasing the risk of something going wrong. Our bodies are too sensitive; they have to be, to do the things we call on them to do. The man who smokes two packs of cigarettes a day for twenty years and develops lung cancer, faces problems which deserve our sympathy, but he has no grounds for asking, "How could God do this to me?" (From *When Bad Things Happen to Good People* by Harold S. Kushner, p. 65. Published by Schocken Books, reprinted by permission of Pantheon Books, a division of Random House, Inc. Copyright © 1981 by Harold S. Kushner.)

"There is a clear and obvious difference between being 'given' a 'thorn in the flesh,' as Paul was, and willfully impaling ourselves on the spears of sin," Elder Neal A. Maxwell profoundly penned. "In the former circumstance, the afflicted may ask 'Why?'—but in the latter situation that is not a useful question to address to anyone but ourselves." (*All These Things Shall Give Thee Experience,* p. 33.)

One of the basic laws of physics is, "For every action there is an equal and opposite reaction." Perhaps this can be compared to how agency, our own and that of others, affects our lives. Every action affects our lives in some manner—sometimes in ways that produce happiness and fulfillment and sometimes in ways that produce pain and frustration. Even inaction, though not necessarily producing a reaction, may affect our lives by causing a forfeiture of reactions or consequences that would be beneficial and productive. Actions and inaction may inflict pain and suffering without being blatantly wicked or sinful by nature. Bruce C. Hafen insightfully distinguished between "acts of independence" that are deliberately sinful in nature and "acts of independence" that can be characterized as "mistakes" or "errors of judgment."

> Some of these actions might also be called sins committed in ignorance. For example, we might act selfishly or insensitively in family relationships, or allow self-interest to cloud our view of another person's needs. There is usually a difference between errors of this nature and serious sin, just as there is a difference among teenagers between foolishness and sin. The law also distinguishes between intentional wrongdoing and carelessness or negligence. Criminal acts, for instance, require proof of conscious criminal intent, suggesting that our moral culpability is higher with deliberate sin than it is with foolish errors. Regardless of our intentions, however, our careless decisions can lead to consequences that harm others as seriously as would a willful decision to hurt them. (*The Broken Heart,* p. 54.)

For example, it may not be sinful to consume chocolate chip cookies or indulge in other fattening "junk" foods, but medical research now indicates that eating certain foods or failing to adhere to principles of proper nutrition can in fact bring about sickness and suffering. I may not be a wicked person by virtue of my dislike for jogging (I subscribe to the view on jogging expressed by BYU president and enthusiastic tennis player Jeffrey R. Holland, who joked that he would take up jogging when the day came that he saw joggers smile); however, my personal avoidance of jogging is an inaction that may cause me to neglect proper physical fitness. Such inaction forfeits the benefits of proper exercise and can ultimately have painful side effects, even to the point of shortening my life. Even actions that are not obviously evil and which may seem innocent can result in tribulation and affliction in our lives. Just as the man who smoked heavily for twenty years brings upon himself lung cancer and has no grounds to claim that God (or someone else) inflicted this trial upon him, so it is with others in so many different types of circumstances.

Rabbi Kushner wrote: "The person who weighs considerably more than he should, and whose heart has to pump blood through miles of additional fat cells and clogged arteries will have to pay the price for that additional strain on his system, and will have no grounds to complain to God. Neither, alas, will the doctor, the clergyman, or the politician who works long hours, seven-day week after seven-day week, in the noblest of causes, but fails to take care of his own health in the process." (*When Bad Things Happen to Good People,* p. 65. See copyright and permission information, p. 25 herein.)

Perhaps this principle of action/reaction and its effect on our lives may be the reason why the living prophets consistently counsel us not only in matters that pertain to our salvation in the celestial kingdom but also in practical matters that can affect the quality of our daily lives. Such counsel has been given in health matters—both physical and emotional—financial and temporal matters, practical family matters, and many other areas of concern. Our response to these inspired counsels can have a powerful effect on our lives. Foolish use of credit cards or incurring unnecessary debt, with their unrelenting drain on family finances, may not keep us out of the celestial kingdom, but such actions can and do exact a heavy toll on our mortal lives. In a similar vein, family home evening, family scripture study, and other worthwhile family practices may not be eternal requisites for entrance into exaltation, but failure to abide the counsel to participate in such activities may cause a forfeiture of significant blessings and of protection from evil influences that can destroy the happiness and security of the home. This loss, in turn, may lead to actions and sins that bring not only emotional distress in mortality but also a loss of the blessings of eternity.

While it is true that much adversity in life results from the use and misuse of agency, we must remember that not all tribulations come as a result of our own actions or those of others. Furthermore, dwelling on how we have been harmed by the sins and deeds of others and condemning ourselves continually for our self-inflicted suffering are counterproductive practices because they interfere with our ability to face the challenges of life with renewed resolve. Blaming ourselves or others for all of our suffering actually stifles the spiritual conditioning that will yield the necessary strength to endure. Elder Marvin J. Ashton declared:

> We must remember that all suffering is not punishment. It is imperative that we do not allow ourselves to be destroyed by the conduct of others.
>
> Sometimes we spend so much time trying to determine what we did wrong in the past to deserve the unpleasant happenings of the moment that we fail to resolve the challenges of the present. . . .
>
> . . . It is important that we not look upon our afflictions as a punishment from God. True, our actions may cause some of our problems, but often there is no evident misconduct that has caused our trials. Just the normal journey through life teaches us that nothing worthwhile comes easy. (" 'If Thou Endure It Well,' " pp. 20, 22.)

Laws of Nature

In the hit Broadway musical *Annie* there is a song that seems to characterize another major source of suffering in life. The song is entitled "It's the Hard-Knock Life." Mortality is indeed full of its share of "hard knocks"—that is just the nature of life. The Savior's expression in the Sermon on the Mount about the impartial and widespread provision of sun and rain (see Matthew 5:45) might also be applied to the unselective nature of mortal misfortune. The Prophet Joseph Smith also explained that suffering and afflictions are an inherent and natural part of life. Speaking of the trials and tribulations associated with the last days and the second coming of the Savior, the Prophet wrote:

> I explained concerning the coming of the Son of Man; also that it is a false idea that the Saints will escape all the judgments, whilst the wicked suffer; for all flesh is subject to suffer, and "the righteous shall hardly escape;" still many of the Saints will escape, for the just shall live by faith; yet many of the righteous shall fall a prey to disease, to pestilence, etc., by reason of the weakness of the flesh, and yet be saved in the Kingdom of God. So that it is an unhallowed principle to say that such and such have transgressed because they have been preyed upon by disease or death, for all flesh is subject to death; and the Savior has said, "Judge not, lest ye be judged." (*Teachings of the Prophet Joseph Smith,* pp. 162–63.)

There is no question that God created, governs, and controls all things—our lives included. But through his creative powers, laws and principles of nature associated with mortality were also established on this earth and set in motion. These laws not only provide great blessings and happiness for his children in mortality but also are a source of opposition necessary for the plan of salvation to fully operate. It is not to be thought, therefore, that everything of an adverse nature that happens in this life was directly willed and/or caused by God. We must allow for the natural occurrences in life, even if they provide us with pain and suffering, for, as the Prophet Joseph stated, "all flesh is subject to suffer." Elder Dean L. Larsen taught:

One of the provisions made for us by our Heavenly Father in his plan for our eternal progress was the nature of the environment into which we come in mortal life. Life on earth is ideally suited to test us and prove us. Laws of cause and effect operate freely. There is opposition in all things. The conditions are designed to bring about the maturation and development essential to the progress of man in this mortal phase of his existence. Earth life is filled with risks. It provides no guarantee for safe passage. It expands our prospects for developing personal accountability.

No one passes through mortality without occasionally experiencing disappointment, heartache, and perhaps even tragedy. Once in a while, for reasons known only to him, the Lord responds to our pleading and prayers of faith and miraculously rescues us from a trial or difficulty. Generally, however, he expects us to cope with them. (*Free to Act,* pp. 28–29.)

It is easy to feel that life is unfair and that we are often undeserving of the tribulations we encounter. This is because life is indeed unfair and inequitable for many reasons. The risk, randomness, and chance involved in living in a mortal world are among those reasons. We often expect to live in a perfect society, and we feel abused or persecuted when we encounter unfairness, opposition, and suffering. It may be that we overlook the fact that this world is a fallen, imperfect, telestial world and has been from the fall of Adam. Just as there were thorns and thistles for Adam and Eve to deal with as a natural part of their mortal sojourn, so adversity and affliction will inevitably be a natural part of our existence. Such opposition and suffering come to the righteous as well as the wicked "by reason of the flesh." Someone once observed, "Expecting life to treat you fairly because you are a good person is like expecting the bull not to charge you because you are a vegetarian."

We must recognize that much of what we suffer in life has little to do with righteousness, wickedness, or God's "will for us" but has a lot to do with the natural and normal conditions of mortality to which we are subjected. Although such mortal risks may seem unfair and cruel, there is greater equality than we often can see with our finite eyes. Some "trials and tribulations come to us merely as a part of living," explained Elder Neal A. Maxwell. "We are not immunized against all inconvenience and difficulties nor against aging. This type of suffering carries its own real challenges, but we do not feel singled out." (*All These Things Shall Give Thee Experience,* p. 30.)

Indeed natural catastrophes and accidents are so prevalent in our world that there seems to be plenty to go around for everyone. In January 1986 the nation watched in horror as a space shuttle exploded in midair, claiming the lives of seven of America's best, brightest, and bravest. Did this event occur because of the wickedness or foolishness of the astronauts or engineers? Of course not! While we may not know all the reasons, perhaps the paramount reason was that it was an accident. In a mortal world machines malfunction and such malfunctions cause accidents, inflict suffering, and even take lives. Airplanes crack open and some passengers are pulled out of the gaping hole to instant death while others, only inches away, are safe in their seats. Were those whose lives were spared more righteous or deserving of life than those who died, or do such tragedies have more to do with mundane, mortal issues like defective aircraft, "metal fatigue," or seat assignment?

There are other calamities that are not related to mechanical operations; rather, they stem from the ironic and inexplicable workings of nature. Tornadoes destroy homes and communities. Sometimes individual houses or neighborhoods appear to be miraculously spared the devastation while nearby locations are leveled. Is this because of righteousness or wickedness, or does it involve the randomness and risk associated with natural laws of weather and geography? Earthquakes, floods, typhoons, mud slides, and avalanches are often characterized as "acts of God" but could more accurately be characterized as "acts of nature." Rabbi Kushner offers this thoughtful explanation for these kinds of events:

> Insurance companies refer to earthquakes, hurricanes, and other natural disasters as "acts of God." I consider that a case of using God's name in vain. I don't believe that an earthquake that kills thousands of innocent victims without reason is an act of God. It is an act of nature. Nature is morally blind, without values. It churns along, following its own laws, not caring who or what gets in the way. But God is not morally blind. I could not worship Him if I thought He was. God stands for justice, for fairness, for compassion. For me, the earthquake is not an "act of God." . . .
>
> If a bridge collapses, if a dam breaks, if a wing falls off an airplane and people die, I cannot see that as God's doing. I cannot believe that God wanted all those people to die at that moment, or that He wanted some of them to die and had no choice but to condemn the others along with them. I believe that these calamities are all acts of nature, and that there is no moral reason for those particular victims to be singled out for punishment. (*When Bad Things Happen to Good People*, pp. 59–60. See copyright and permission information, p. 25 herein.)

The laws of nature also affect us in less dramatic ways. Sickness, disease, and all manner of ailments come to the human family by reason of the Fall. Our bodies begin to deteriorate and die as soon as we are born. The Apostle Paul referred to the mortal nature of the human body, with all of its inherent problems, when he spoke of the resurrection as being a transformation of a "corruptible" body to one of "incorruption" (see 1 Corinthians 15:53). Many of the physical hardships we suffer in mortality are merely natural by-products of the essential workings of the plan of salvation. "Laws of nature do not make exceptions for nice people," writes Harold Kushner. "I don't know why one person gets sick, and another does not, but I can only assume that some natural laws which we don't understand are at work." (*When Bad Things Happen to Good People*, p. 60. See copyright and permission information, p. 25 herein.) This may explain one of the reasons why even Jesus, the Sinless One, was not exempt from discomforts and distress, sicknesses and suffering.

LDS doctrine, of course, recognizes that divine intervention can occur, but the following comments by Rabbi Kushner emphasize the impartiality of natural laws:

> Laws of nature treat everyone alike. They do not make exceptions for good people or for useful people. If a man enters a house where someone has a contagious disease, he runs the risk of catching that disease. It makes no difference why he is in the house. He may be a doctor or a burglar; disease germs cannot tell the difference. . . .
>
> Laws of nature do not make exceptions for nice people. A bullet has no conscience; neither does a malignant tumor or an automobile gone out of control. That is why good people get sick and get hurt as much as anyone. . . . God does not reach down to interrupt the workings of laws of nature to protect the righteous from harm. . . .
>
> And really, how could we live in this world if He did? . . . Would this be a better world, if certain people were immune to laws of nature because God favored them, while the rest of us had to fend for ourselves?
>
> Let us suppose, . . . for purposes of argument, that I was one of those righteous people to whom God would not

let anything bad happen, because I was an observant, charitable person with a young family, spending my life helping people. What would that mean? Would I be able to go out in my shirtsleeves in cold weather and not get sick, because God would prevent the workings of nature from doing me harm? Could I cross streets against the lights in the face of heavy traffic, and not be injured? Could I jump out of high windows when I was in too much of a hurry to wait for an elevator, and not hurt myself? A world in which good people suffer from the same natural dangers that others do causes problems. But a world in which good people were immune to those laws would cause even more problems. (*When Bad Things Happen to Good People,* pp. 58–59. See copyright and permission information, p. 25 herein.)

Acts of God

The third source of tribulation in life could *accurately* be characterized as "acts of God." These occurrences are designed and brought about by God in a purposeful manner to further his work and to bless the lives of his children, though to many the idea that a loving Father would cause his own children to suffer may seem a problematic paradox. While we cannot, with our present veiled and finite understanding, fully comprehend all of the purposes of God, we can begin to recognize the merciful hand of God in our own lives and adversities. This increased perception comes to us gradually—"line upon line, precept upon precept"—through the inspired words of the scriptures and living prophets, as well as through personal experience and the private promptings of the Comforter.

This third cause of adversity is distinct from yet integrally connected with each of the other two causes—agency and natural law. In this case God may not only allow agency and nature to run their own unique courses but also use them to actively intervene in the lives of his children—both collectively and individually—to bring about his purposes. Elder Spencer W. Kimball, in his address "Tragedy or Destiny?" said: "Did the Lord cause the man to suffer a heart attack? Was the death of the missionary untimely? Answer, if you can. I cannot, for though I know God has a major role in our lives, I do not know how much he causes to happen and how much he merely permits." (In *Faith Precedes the Miracle*, p. 96.) Acts of God may come to us in the form of "customized adversity," or they may be the "acts of men" or "acts of nature" which God permits and utilizes for his own purposes. The scriptures testify that the Lord sometimes uses the principles of agency and nature to further his own work of bringing to pass "the immortality and eternal life of man" (Moses 1:39). In modern revelation the Lord has said:

> How oft have I called upon you by the mouth of my servants, and by the ministering of angels, and by mine own voice, and by the voice of *thunderings,* and by the voice of *lightnings,* and by the voice of *tempests,* and by the voice of *earthquakes,* and great *hailstorms,* and by the voice of *famines* and *pestilences of every kind,* and by the great sound of a trump, and by the voice of judgment, and by the voice of mercy all the day long, and by the voice of glory and honor and the riches of eternal life, and would have saved you with an everlasting salvation, but ye would not! (D&C 43:25, italics added.)

In addition a prophet in our own day has confirmed the causal relationship that can exist between man's unrighteousness and God's use of the workings of nature. President Spencer W. Kimball in the April 1977 general conference declared, "The Lord uses the weather sometimes to discipline his people for the violation of his laws" ("The Lord Expects His Saints to Follow the Commandments," p. 4).

Because the Lord not only allows agency and nature to operate freely but also employs these laws to meet his objectives, it becomes extremely difficult to ascertain which of these three main causes of suffering is in operation in any given circumstance. "To pretend that the boundary lines between types of suffering can be drawn with clinical precision and that demarcation is possible in all circumstances would be a mistake," cautioned Elder Neal A. Maxwell. "Moreover, the interplay between the various forms of suffering makes them interactive." (*All These Things Shall Give Thee Experience,* p. 33.)

Although we may not completely comprehend *how* God carries out his will through our adversity, the scriptures help elevate our understanding of *why* he permits and even causes pain and suffering to become our traveling companions on our sojourn through life.

Redemptive Reminders

C. S. Lewis, in his reflective work *The Problem of Pain,* characterized pain and suffering as God's "megaphone to rouse a deaf world." Adversity grabs our attention and turns our hearts to God. "Pain insists upon being attended to," Lewis wrote. "God whispers to us in our pleasures, speaks in our conscience, but shouts in our pains." (P. 93.) This image of God using the "megaphone" of pain to turn the attention of mankind to him and his higher way of life is evident throughout the scriptures. Many scriptural passages witness of the merciful designs of God in allowing and causing anguish and adversity, sorrow and suffering. In his abridged account of Lamanite and Nephite history, Mormon added his own observations and editorial comments about the roles of prosperity, pride, affliction, and adversity.

> And thus we can behold how false, and also the unsteadiness of the hearts of the children of men; yea, we can see that the Lord in his great infinite goodness doth bless and prosper those who put their trust in him.
>
> Yea, and we may see at the very time when he doth prosper his people, yea, in the increase of their fields, their flocks and their herds, and in gold, and in silver, and in all manner of precious things of every kind and art; . . . yea, and in fine, doing all things for the welfare and happiness of his people; yea, then is the time that they do harden their hearts, and do forget the Lord their God, and do trample under their feet the Holy One—yea, and this because of their ease, and their exceedingly great prosperity.
>
> And thus we see that except the Lord doth chasten his people with many afflictions, yea, except he doth visit them with death and with terror, and with famine and with all manner of pestilence, they will not remember him. (Helaman 12:1–3.)

King Benjamin likewise taught of the prodding purpose of trials and tribulations when he taught his son Mosiah and gave him charge of the sacred records. He explained that Lehi's family, as they traveled in the wilderness, "were smitten with famine and sore afflictions, to stir them up in remembrance of their duty" (Mosiah 1:17). God's use of adversity to turn the hearts and minds of his children to him was also a recurring theme of Old Testament writers (see Leviticus 26; 1 Kings 8:35–36; Hosea 5:15; Isaiah 30:20; 48:10; 2 Chronicles 20:9). Perhaps the most profound and poignant illustration comes from the poetic pen of the Psalmist. Describing the rebelliousness of the children of Israel after the Exodus, he wrote:

> And they sinned yet more against [the Lord] by pro-
> voking the most High in the wilderness.
>
> And they tempted God in their heart by asking meat
> for their lust. . . .
>
> And he let it fall in the midst of their camp, round
> about their habitations.
>
> So they did eat, and were well filled: for he gave them
> their own desire;
>
> They were not estranged from their lust. But while
> their meat was yet in their mouths,
>
> The wrath of God came upon them, and slew the fat-
> test of them, and smote down the chosen men of Israel.
>
> For all this they sinned still, and believed not for his
> wondrous works.
>
> Therefore their days did he consume in vanity, and
> their years in trouble.
>
> When he slew them, then they sought him: and they
> returned and enquired early after God.
>
> And they remembered that God was their rock, and
> the high God their redeemer. (Psalm 78:17–18, 28–35.)

It may seem rather cruel that the Lord would use such seemingly harsh means to ensure that we "always remember him." We may securely feel that we will not forget him, even in ease and prosperity, and that we will always be faithful and devoted. While it may be possible to remain true without severe suffering, the Lord's metaphor of a camel trying to go through the eye of a needle seems to suggest the incompatibility of living a life of ease and being a disciple of Christ (see JST, Matthew 19:23–26). All too often we may be like the rich young man who inquired of Jesus what he must do to obtain eternal life (see Matthew 19:16–22). Even if we don't selfishly cling to earthly treasures as the rich young man did, like him we may still want our lives to remain pleasant, peaceful, and prosperous while we follow the Master with complete devotion. The danger with this attitude is that it is often a cover for hidden allegiances to the things of the world, allegiances that may divert or even prevent us from complete allegiance to the Master (see Matthew 6:21–24). We may never discover where our *true* allegiance lies until we, like the rich young man, are forced to choose.

Nephi warned of potential spiritual pitfalls that come with the collective and individual attitude that "All is well in Zion" (see 2 Nephi 28:21). This deceptive feeling of "carnal security" does not develop suddenly, but over a period of time when life seems to be going smoothly. During seasons of ease and comfort there may come a quiet, almost unnoticeable tendency to become less dependent upon the Lord and more secure in self and in the things of the world. Of this universal human phenomenon and the need for God's merciful yet painful intervention, C. S. Lewis observed:

> If the first and lowest operation of pain shatters the illusion that all is well, the second shatters the illusion that what we have, whether good or bad in itself, is our own and enough for us. Everyone has noticed how hard it is to turn our thoughts to God when everything is going well with us. We "have all we want" is a terrible saying when "all" does not include God. We find God an interruption. As St. Augustine says somewhere, "God wants to give us something, but cannot, because our hands are full— there's nowhere for Him to put it." Or as a friend of mine said, "We regard God as an airman regards his parachute; it's there for emergencies but he hopes he'll never have to use it." Now God, who has made us, knows what we are and that our happiness lies in Him. Yet we will not seek it in Him as long as He leaves us any other resort where it can even plausibly be looked for. While what we call "our own life" remains agreeable we will not surrender it to Him. What then can God do in our interests but

make "our own life" less agreeable to us, and take away the plausible sources of false happiness? It is just here, where God's providence seems at first to be most cruel, that the Divine humility, the stooping down of the Highest, most deserves praise. (*The Problem of Pain*, pp. 95–96.)

In a personal way I discovered what the scriptures (and C. S. Lewis) really mean when they speak of adversity and affliction causing us to remember God and turn our hearts more fully to him. Our two-year-old child was injured in a freak accident. She fell off the top of our parked car (which she was using as a dance stage), landing on her head on the concrete driveway. Although we could see she was hurt and she would not stop screaming, my wife and I did not at first know how serious such an injury could be. It was not until we observed the concern of our pediatrician that we became alarmed. The pediatrician informed us that there could be brain damage and that we had to get our little girl to the nearby trauma center immediately. She called for an ambulance to transport us to the hospital and also called ahead to have a neurosurgeon await our arrival. Amidst this panic and pandemonium I laid my hands on our daughter's head and gave her a priesthood blessing. In an anguish of soul I had never before known, I pleaded with the Lord as I drove behind the speeding ambulance. My faith and prayers at that moment were much different than they had been that morning as I knelt by my bed or as we knelt in family prayer. Even though we had earnestly tried to remember the Lord, I discovered a vast difference between "saying prayers" and "crying unto the Lord." In this moment of distress my soul became more keenly attuned to the things of the Spirit. Amidst the anxiety and uncertainty resulting from our daughter's accident there came into my life a spiritual soul-stretching that was both painful and beneficial. I learned that spiritual strength, like physical strength, is only increased through resistance, difficulty, and exertion. "Affliction comes to us all, not to make us sad, but sober; not to make us sorry, but wise," wrote Henry Ward Beecher. "It is trial that proves one thing weak and another strong. . . . A cobweb is as good as the mightiest cable when there is no strain upon it." (In Richard L. Evans, *Richard Evans' Quote Book*, p. 56.)

Perhaps inherent in the spiritual and physical side effects of the fall of Adam is the natural desire for ease and comfort—a desire which is antithetical to spiritual growth. Because we cannot (or at least do not) sufficiently turn to God both in our attitudes and our actions, the Lord uses the "megaphone" of adversity and affliction to shepherd us to greener pastures and keep us under his watchful care (see Psalm 23). In times of tribulation we often resist this compassion and love, because we cannot see beyond the perspective of the "natural man" and discern the purposes of God in our present pains. "[Tribulation] is not an end in itself," wrote President Joseph F. Smith. "Calamities are only permitted by a merciful Father, in order to bring about redemption. Behind the fearful storms of judgment, which often strike the just and the unjust alike, . . . there arises bright and clear the dawn of the day of salvation." ("The Lesson in Natural Calamities," p. 651.) Just as we must rely on a Savior to redeem us from the spiritual and physical deaths imposed by the Fall, we must also rely on the "acts of God"—as painful and difficult as they may be—to help us remember him and our duty to him, and to help us achieve our spiritual potential. Trials and tribulations that are "acts of God"—whether allowed to occur through the natural operation of man's agency and the laws of nature or specifically tailored and set in motion—are redemptive, not punitive, in purpose.

Spiritual Remodeling

Adversity—God's painful megaphone—as a redemptive reminder of who he is and how we must totally depend on him is much like the loud ringing of a school bell. It grabs our attention, startles us out of our comfort zone, awakens us from our daydreaming, and beckons us to commence the important task of learning. The school bell serves as an attention-getting signal which summons us to class, but the real education is obtained not from the school bell but from the schoolmaster. Our afflictions—the God-permitted and God-created, purposeful tribulations we experience—are not only like the summoning school bell but also, in a broader and more significant way, like the schoolmaster who patiently and sometimes even sternly shapes and stretches each student to his fullest potential. The Lord himself accentuated this soul-shaping role of adversity when he declared: "Verily, thus saith the Lord unto you whom I love, and *whom I love I also chasten that their sins may be forgiven,* for with the chastisement I prepare a way for their deliverance in all things out of temptation, and I have loved you—wherefore, ye must needs be chastened." (D&C 95:1-2, italics added.)

Because of his infinite love for each of us, God uses heartaches and hardships to chasten us and strengthen us. This may seem contradictory if we define the word *chasten* only in terms of punishment or castigation. The broader meaning of the word adds such important elements as "to instruct, teach, restrain, moderate" and the spiritually significant terms "to purify and refine." The definitions help us to see God as the dedicated Schoolmaster, utilizing adversities in our lives as object lessons to instruct us, his students, and to help us to learn by experience lessons that could not be obtained merely from books and chalkboards. President Joseph F. Smith, who knew much affliction and heartache in his own life, explained the instructive value of adversity. "Severe, natural calamities are visited upon men by the Lord for the good of his children, to quicken their devotion to others, and to bring out their better natures. . . . They are the heralds and tokens of his final judgment, and the schoolmasters to teach the people to prepare themselves by righteous living for the coming of the Savior." (*Gospel Doctrine*, p. 55.)

Much more significant, however, than the view of God as a schoolmaster teaching his class is the understanding that God is our literal, loving Father, who compassionately helps to purify us and to spiritually shape us into the kind of beings that he and the Savior, our Elder Brother, are. The Apostle Paul taught: "My son, despise not thou the chastening of the Lord, nor faint when thou art rebuked of him: For whom the Lord loveth he chasteneth, and scourgeth every son whom he receiveth. If ye endure chastening, God dealeth with you as with sons; for what son is he whom the father chasteneth not? But if ye be without chastisement, whereof all are partakers, then are ye bastards, and not sons." (Hebrews 12:5-8.)

This God-designed and God-desired chastening that is associated with life's tests and ordeals involves a stripping away of undesirable traits and false allegiances. The scriptures speak of this process as the "refiner's fire" (see Malachi 3:2). Elder James E. Faust explained in the April 1979 general conference how adversity and affliction, as a refiner's fire, indeed *chasten*—or in the truest sense of the word—*purify*.

In the pain, the agony, and the heroic endeavors of life, we pass through a refiner's fire, and the insignificant and the unimportant in our lives can melt away like dross and make our faith bright, intact, and strong. In this way the divine image can be mirrored from the soul. It is part of the purging toll exacted of some to become acquainted with God. In the agonies of life, we seem to listen better to the faint, godly whisperings of the Divine Shepherd.

Into every life there come the painful, despairing days of adversity and buffeting. There seems to be a full measure of anguish, sorrow, and often heartbreak for everyone, including those who earnestly seek to do right and be faithful. The thorns that prick, that stick in the flesh, that hurt, often change lives which seem robbed of significance and hope. This change comes about through a refining process which often seems cruel and hard. In this way the soul can become like soft clay in the hands of the Master in building lives of faith, usefulness, beauty, and strength. For some, the refiner's fire causes a loss of belief and faith in God, but those with eternal perspective understand that such refining is part of the perfection process. ("The Refiner's Fire," p. 53.)

Refining implies a melting away or an elimination of things undesirable and/or unnecessary. Certainly this is a central reason for the acts of God in our lives, but there is another equally desirable outcome. After the refining there must also be a reshaping or reconstruction. Just as that which is undesirable needs to be eliminated, those traits that are essential to our happiness and spiritual progress need to be added and reinforced. Adversity and affliction can become important tools whereby this spiritual remodeling may be accomplished. "No possible degree of holiness or heroism which has ever been recorded of the greatest saints is beyond what He is determined to produce in every one of us in the end," observed C. S. Lewis.

The job will not be completed in this life: but He means to get us as far as possible before death.

That is why we must not be surprised if we are in for a rough time. When a man turns to Christ and seems to be getting on pretty well (in the sense that some of his bad habits are now corrected), he often feels that it would now be natural if things went fairly smoothly. When troubles come along—illnesses, money troubles, new kinds of temptation—he is disappointed. These things, he feels, might have been necessary to rouse him and make him repent in his bad old days; but why now? Because God is forcing him . . . into situations where he will have to be very much braver, or more patient, or more loving, than he ever dreamed of being before. It seems to us all unnecessary: but that is because we have not yet had the slightest notion of the tremendous thing He means to make of us.

To further illustrate this point, Lewis paraphrased a parable of his mentor, the great religious thinker George MacDonald, who compared the way God mercifully utilizes pain and suffering in our lives to a contractor's remodeling of a house.

Imagine yourself as a living house. God comes in to rebuild that house. At first, perhaps, you can understand what He is doing. He is getting the drains right and stopping the leaks in the roof and so on: you knew that those jobs needed doing and so you are not surprised. But presently He starts knocking the house about in a way that hurts abominably and does not seem to make sense. What on earth is He up to? The explanation is that He is building quite a different house from the one you thought of—throwing out a new wing here, putting on an extra floor there, running up towers, making courtyards. You thought you were going to be made into a decent little cottage: but He is building a palace. He intends to come and live in it Himself. (*Mere Christianity*, pp. 173–74.)

Every remodeling job has its accompanying cost and inconvenience. Soul-stretching, spiritual remodeling is no different; it has its own cost in pain and sorrow, yet it may also yield a palatial enlargement of our souls, an enhancement of our spirituality, and a remaking of our very beings in the image of him who "hath descended below" all suffering and pain (D&C 122:8).

Spiritual Sustenance

The prophet Isaiah, in a prophecy regarding the redemption of Israel, used a most interesting phrase concerning the pitfalls and punishments that his people would yet suffer: "And though the Lord give you *the bread of adversity, and the water of affliction,* yet shall not thy teachers [the Lord] be removed into a corner any more, but thine eyes shall see thy teachers" (Isaiah 30:20, italics added). It is interesting to note that the prophet acknowledges that God does indeed at times give his people troubles. These "acts of God" were characterized by Isaiah not with negative terms such as *pain* or *sorrow* but rather with the deeply symbolic terms *bread* and *water.* Adversity and affliction are purposely portrayed in a different light than that in which we ordinarily view them.

To the Israelites, bread and water were not only significant symbols of physical nourishment and life sustenance but also symbols of Jehovah's merciful and miraculous life-saving interventions. When the Camp of Israel faced famine and starvation during the exodus from Egypt, they were sustained and nourished, every day of their forty-year journey, by manna—bread from heaven (see Exodus 16; Deuteronomy 8:3, 16). When they faced desperate thirst, the Lord commanded Moses to strike a rock, and thirst-quenching, life-sustaining water miraculously flowed forth (see Exodus 17; Numbers 20:7–11; Psalm 78:15–16). Perhaps Isaiah, ever speaking in richly endowed symbols, was alluding to these examples of divinely dispensed bread and water when he spoke of adversity and affliction.

Bread and water, as symbols of sustenance, take on even greater spiritual significance in the teachings of Jesus. At Jacob's well in Shechem, Jesus taught the Samaritan woman: "Whosoever drinketh of this water [from Jacob's well] shall thirst again: but whosoever drinketh of the water that I shall give him shall never thirst; but the water that I shall give him shall be in him a well of water springing up into everlasting life" (John 4:13–14). Shortly thereafter he reminded his disciples of the ancient miracle of the manna provided to their fathers, and then he taught: "I am that bread of life. . . . I am the living bread which came down from heaven: if any man eat of this bread, he shall live for ever: and the bread that I will give is my flesh, which I will give for the life of the world." (John 6:48, 51.)

Adversity and affliction, allowed and bestowed by an omniscient Father, are as essential for our spiritual health and well-being as bread and water are to our physical welfare. Perhaps there are no greater theological symbols of spiritual life than bread and water. Each week these symbols focus our attention on the Savior and his life-saving and life-giving sacrifice. When we think of adversity and affliction in terms of "bread from heaven" and "living waters," not only can we see that tribulation is given by God to attract our attention, turn our hearts to him, and spiritually reshape us, but also we recognize that in reality there is neither spiritual life nor, ultimately, eternal life without partaking of the "bread of adversity" and the "water of affliction." Suffering and sorrow, pain and problems, trials and tribulations are not just incidental sideshows in life or optional character-shaping experiences —they are essentials for our own progress and are imperative in the operation of the plan for our salvation.

CHAPTER THREE

Adversity and the Purposes of Life

In the account of Job we learn implicitly that when the plan of salvation was presented in the premortal Grand Council "all the sons of God shouted for joy" (Job 38:7). Amidst the jubilation of these spirits at the prospects of earth life, there must have been a degree of apprehension and anxiety in anticipation of the challenges as well as the opportunities of mortality. No doubt each of us had been taught and prepared for our mortal sojourn. Such teaching perhaps included discussions of life's difficulties and hardships as well as its blessings and exciting possibilities. Undoubtedly we learned of the integral role adversity and affliction would play in our own individual lives and in the overall operation of the plan of salvation.

Here on earth the veil of forgetfulness has been drawn over our minds, and we have forgotten those discussions

and premortal teachings. We are not left on our own, however, without doctrinal instruction and spiritual comfort.
Our Father in Heaven has mercifully revealed many important explanations to his prophets as to why we are on
earth and what we must do to be faithful amidst affliction
in this second estate. "God has placed us here upon the
earth to accomplish important purposes," declared President George Q. Cannon. "These purposes have been in
part revealed unto us. Probably it is not possible for men
and women in this mortal state of existence to comprehend
all the designs of God connected with man's existence
upon the earth; but much has been revealed upon this subject to us as a people." (*Gospel Truth*, p. 10.) The scriptures and latter-day prophets testify of life's three main
purposes—obtaining physical bodies, being tested and
tried, and gaining beneficial experience. These three goals
are simply unattainable without adversity. Of the faith-
testing and character-building role of adversity and its relationship to the plan of salvation, Elder Spencer W. Kimball taught:

> Some become bitter when oft-repeated prayers seem
> unanswered. Some lose faith and turn sour when solemn
> administrations by holy men seem to be ignored and no
> restoration seems to come from repeated prayer circles.
> But if all the sick were healed, if all the righteous were
> protected and the wicked destroyed, the whole program of
> the Father would be annulled. . . .
>
> If pain and sorrow and total punishment immediately
> followed the doing of evil, no soul would repeat a mis-
> deed. If joy and peace and rewards were instantaneously
> given the doer of good, there could be no evil—all would
> do good and not because of the rightness of doing good.
> There would be no test of strength, no development of
> character, no growth of powers, no free agency. . . . There
> would also be an absence of joy, success, resurrection,

eternal life, and godhood. (*Teachings of Spencer W. Kimball,* p. 77.)

Physical Bodies

The scriptures clearly teach that we cannot lay hold upon exaltation and a fulness of joy without coming to earth and receiving mortal, physical bodies (see D&C 45:17; 93:33–34; 138:15–18). We learned in the premortal councils in heaven that having a physical body is an imperative part of the plan of salvation. Elder George Q. Cannon explained:

> It was necessary that a probation should be given to man. The courts of heaven were thronged with spirits that desired tabernacles. They wanted to come and obtain fleshly tabernacles as their Father had done. Their progenitors, the race of Gods with whom they associated and from whom they have descended, had had the privilege of coming on earthly probations and receiving tabernacles, which by obedience they had been able to redeem. Hence, I say, the courts of heaven were thronged with spirits anxious to take upon themselves tabernacles of flesh, agreeing to come forth and be tested and tried in order that they might receive exaltation. (*Gospel Truth,* p. 21.)

The Prophet Joseph Smith taught that "no person can have this salvation except through a tabernacle" (*Teachings of the Prophet Joseph Smith,* p. 297). The Prophet also taught that having a physical body is a key element in our proving ourselves and obtaining happiness: "We came to this earth that we might have a body and present it pure before God in the celestial kingdom. The great principle of happiness consists in having a body. The devil has no body, and herein is his punishment. He is pleased when he can obtain the tabernacle of man, and when cast out by the Savior he asked to go into the herd of swine, showing that he would prefer a swine's body to having none." (*Teachings of the Prophet Joseph Smith,* p. 181.)

The key phrase in Joseph's statement is, "present it pure before God." Learning to let the spirit control the fleshly tabernacle of our body is one of life's most important and difficult struggles. "The great object of our existence is to have the mind and the spirit right, the feelings and passions under control," declared Elder Orson Pratt, "to have the mortal man that dwells within led and dictated by the Holy Spirit" (In *Journal of Discourses* 8:311). Being born into this world with a body is the easy part—controlling and purifying it is the daunting task. But it is with this very task—this requirement for salvation—that adversity and affliction can become "helpful." Burdens and encumbrances of a physical nature often provide the very opportunities to gain spiritual control of the temporal body. The painful, often debilitating, physical challenges of life are to a degree universal by reason of the mortal condition. Even prophets and Apostles have had to face these vexations and recognize them as part of the plan. The Apostle Paul spoke of a "warfare" between the physical and spiritual parts of his own nature:

> For I know that in me (that is, in my flesh,) dwelleth no good thing: for to will is present with me; but how to perform that which is good I find not.
>
> For the good that I would I do not: but the evil which I would not, that I do.
>
> Now if I do that I would not, it is no more I that do it, but sin that dwelleth in me.
>
> I find then a law, that, when I would do good, evil is present with me.
>
> For I delight in the law of God after the inward man [or spirit]:

> But I see another law in my members [or body], warring against the law of my mind [spirit], and bringing me into captivity to the law of sin which is in my members.
>
> O wretched man that I am! who shall deliver me from the body of this death? (Romans 7:18–24.)

This continual struggle between flesh and spirit, which is universal to mankind and essential to spiritual growth and development, was also described by Nephi:

> Behold, my soul delighteth in the things of the Lord; and my heart pondereth continually upon the things which I have seen and heard.
>
> Nevertheless, notwithstanding the great goodness of the Lord, in showing me his great and marvelous works, my heart exclaimeth: O wretched man that I am! Yea, my heart sorroweth because of my flesh; my soul grieveth because of mine iniquities.
>
> I am encompassed about, because of the temptations and the sins which do so easily beset me.
>
> And when I desire to rejoice, my heart groaneth because of my sins; nevertheless, I know in whom I have trusted. (2 Nephi 4:16–19.)

Paul's and Nephi's descriptions of this temporal tugging between the body and the spirit could perhaps be compared to the challenges faced by a long-distance runner. Marathon runners often use the term *wall* to describe the feeling they encounter during the race when their physical energies are spent and it becomes extremely painful and almost impossible to continue. At that crucial point a mental or even spiritual power or desire must dictate the response of the body in order for the runner to complete the race. People in the world typically characterize that inner strength using words such as ''guts'' or ''willpower.'' In a more fundamental and spiritual sense, it could be characterized as letting the spirit control and give life and energy to the body.

Whether brought on by agency, natural means, or the customized designs of God, our mortal afflictions provide each of us with opportunities to learn to let spiritual powers and traits become more dominant in our lives. Infirmities that may severely limit or even debilitate the physical body often bring about a profound personal development as the spiritual will gathers strength and triumphs over the natural man. Elder Spencer W. Kimball explained that when the physical body becomes less dominant through illness, accident, or aging, spiritual qualities can more easily surface and benefit us:

> I'm grateful that my priesthood power is limited and used as the Lord sees fit to use it. I don't want to heal all the sick—for sickness sometimes is a great blessing. People become angels through sickness.
>
> Have you ever seen someone who has been helpless for so long that he has divested himself of every envy and jealousy and ugliness in his whole life, and who has perfected his life? I have.
>
> Being human, we would expel from our lives, sorrow, distress, physical pain, and mental anguish and assure ourselves of continual ease and [physical] comfort. But if we closed the doors upon such, we might be evicting our greatest friends and benefactors. Suffering can make saints of people as they learn patience, long-suffering, and self-mastery. The sufferings of our Savior were part of his education. (*Teachings of Spencer W. Kimball*, pp. 167–68.)

Afflictions associated with the physical body not only can, as President Joseph F. Smith said, "bring out our better natures" but also can serve as "schoolmasters" of spiritual self-mastery. Brigham Young taught:

When you are tempted, buffetted, and step out of the way inadvertently; when you are overtaken in a fault, or commit an overt act unthinkingly; when you are full of evil passion, and wish to yield to it, then stop and let the spirit, which God has put into your tabernacles, take the lead. If you do that, I will promise that you will overcome all evil, and obtain eternal lives. But many, very many, let the spirit yield to the body, and are overcome and destroyed. . . .

But let the body rise up with its passions, with the fallen nature pertaining to it, and let the spirit yield to it, your destruction is sure. On the other hand, let the spirit take the lead, and bring the body and its passions into subjection, and you are safe. (In *Journal of Discourses* 2:256.)

Suffering as a result of physical maladies, as well as a result of the ongoing "warfare" between body and spirit, may help to teach us obedience even as it did the Savior (see Hebrews 5:8–9).

Testing

Numerous scriptural passages, both ancient and modern, identify testing as one of the primary purposes for man's mortal sojourn. Abraham saw in vision the premortal world and heard God declare the purpose of earth life. "And there stood one among them that was like unto God, and he said unto those who were with him: We will go down, for there is space there, and we will take of these materials, and we will make an earth whereon these may dwell; and we will prove them herewith, to see if they will do all things whatsoever the Lord their God shall command them." (Abraham 3:24–25.)

Certainly Abraham in his own life learned the deep significance of those words when he faced his own heart-wrenching test of faithfulness with the command to offer his own son Isaac as a sacrifice to the Lord (see Genesis 22:1-18; Hebrews 11:17-19). Other prophets have also learned through experience and revelation the absolute necessity of the testing and trial of faith in the mortal experience. Job declared from his own supreme suffering and profound personal perplexities, "But [God] knoweth the way that I take: when he hath tried me, I shall come forth as gold" (Job 23:10).

Through the Prophet Joseph Smith the Lord commanded the early Saints: "And I give unto you a commandment, that ye shall forsake all evil and cleave unto all good, that ye shall live by every word which proceedeth forth out of the mouth of God. For he will give unto the faithful line upon line, precept upon precept; and I will try you and prove you herewith." (D&C 98:11-12.)

Amidst the hardships of crossing the plains and the trial of faith that such suffering produced, Brigham Young learned from the Lord the purposeful and beneficial nature of life's tests. "My people must be tried in all things, that they may be prepared to receive the glory that I have for them, even the glory of Zion; and he that will not bear chastisement is not worthy of my kingdom" (D&C 136:31).

Life for each of us has its full share of trying moments. Whether such moments are self-inflicted, perpetrated upon us by others, or the natural occurrences of life is really irrelevant. Even when they may seem undeserved, adversities and afflictions, whatever their source, are integral ingredients in the imperative trial of one's faith. Elder Neal A. Maxwell has observed the following concerning this significant relationship between adversity and testing:

"Nevertheless the Lord seeth fit to chasten his people; yea, he trieth their patience and their faith" (Mosiah 23:21).

This very sobering declaration of divine purpose ought to keep us on spiritual alert as to life's adversities.

Irony is the hard crust on the bread of adversity. Irony can try both our faith and our patience. Irony can be a particularly bitter form of such chastening because it involves disturbing incongruity. It involves outcomes in violation of our expectations. We see the best laid plans laid waste. . . .

Words then issue, such as Why me? Why this? Why now? Of course, these words may give way to subsequent spiritual composure. Sometimes, however, such words precede bitter inconsolability, and then it is a surprisingly short distance between disappointment and bitterness. . . .

Irony may involve not only unexpected suffering but also undeserved suffering. We feel we deserved better, and yet we fared worse. . . .

. . . We forget that, by their very nature, tests are unfair. ("Irony: The Crust on the Bread of Adversity," pp. 62–63.)

Thus tests and trials may come from a variety of sources, yet still be utilized to try our faith and test our loyalty to God. The Prophet Joseph Smith taught that in order for a person to fulfill the ultimate purpose of the plan of salvation and have his calling and election made sure, he must be "thoroughly proved," and God must find "that the man is determined to serve Him at all hazards" (*Teachings of the Prophet Joseph Smith*, p. 150). Prophets have testified that above and beyond the natural bumps and bruises we experience as we travel the road of life, there are additional "individualized" troubles and torments designed to prove each of us personally. "In time each person will receive a 'customized challenge' to determine his dedication to God,'' Elder Maxwell confirmed (as quoted in *Daily Universe,* BYU, Provo, 7 October 1983, p. 11). President John Taylor reported what Joseph Smith had taught concerning the role of these painfully personal tests in obtaining salvation: "I heard the Prophet Joseph say, in speaking to the Twelve on one occasion: 'You will have all kinds of trials to pass through. And it is quite necessary for you to be tried as it was for Abraham and other men of God, and (said he) God will feel after you, and He will take hold of you and wrench your very heart strings, and if you cannot stand it you will not be fit for an inheritance in the Celestial Kingdom of God.' '' (In *Journal of Discourses* 24:197.)

Faith such as the ancients had requires testing such as they had. Sometimes those Abrahamic tests may be so unnerving as to cause us to cry out in agony and in a feeling of abandonment. "Why hast thou forsaken me?" was the outcry of the Savior at the painful pinnacle of his supreme suffering. After the martyrdom of Joseph and Hyrum at Carthage their mother, Lucy Mack Smith, also implored in the agony of her soul, "My God, my God, why hast thou forsaken this family!" (*History of Joseph Smith,* p. 324.) That feeling of forsakenness may be part of the test of our full faith in and total dependence upon the Lord. We may never fully know the depth of our trust in the Lord and our commitment to him until we feel totally alone in our suffering. C. S. Lewis, who watched his beloved wife slowly die of cancer, wrote a journal in which he recorded the struggles, the insights, and ultimately the renewed faith that came to him through this experience. The following excerpts reveal how his faith matured as he faced the reality of his own Abrahamic test:

Where is God? This is one of the most disquieting symptoms. When you are happy, so happy that you have no sense of needing Him, so happy that you are tempted to feel His claims upon you as an interruption, if you remember yourself and turn to Him with gratitude and praise, you will be—or so it feels—welcomed with open arms. But go to Him when your need is desperate, when all other help is vain, and what do you find? A door slammed in your face, and a sound of bolting and double bolting on the inside. After that, silence. You may as well turn away. The longer you wait, the more emphatic the silence will become. There are no lights in the windows. It might be an empty house. Was it ever inhabited? It seemed so once. And that seeming was as strong as this. What can this mean? Why is He so present a commander in our time of prosperity and so very absent a help in time of trouble?

You never know how much you really believe anything until its truth or falsehood becomes a matter of life and death to you. It is easy to say you believe a rope to be strong and sound as long as you are merely using it to cord a box. But suppose you had to hang by that rope over a precipice. Wouldn't you then first discover how much you really trusted it? . . . Only a real risk tests the reality of a belief.

Bridge-players tell me that there must be some money on the game, "or else people won't take it seriously." Apparently it's like that. Your bid—for God or no God, for a good God or the Cosmic Sadist, for eternal life or nonentity—will not be serious if nothing much is staked on it. And you will never discover how serious it was until the stakes are raised horribly high; until you find that you are playing not for counters or for sixpences but for every penny you have in the world. Nothing less will shake a man—or at any rate a man like me—out of his merely verbal thinking and his merely notional beliefs. He has to be knocked silly before he comes to his senses. (Excerpts from *A Grief Observed* by C. S. Lewis, pp. 4–5, 25, 43. Copyright © 1961 by N. W. Clerk. Reprinted by permission of HarperCollins Publishers.)

The test of adversity—the kind of test possibly accompanied by a feeling of forsakenness—powerfully strips away false faith and superficial spirituality. Of the soul-saving, faith-producing value of tests and trials, Moroni declared, "For ye receive no witness until after the trial of your faith" (Ether 12:6). Only when we hang by the thread of our own testimony do we find out what we really believe, to whom we really are loyal, and what spiritual substance really fills our souls. The exact nature of such saving tests of faith will not necessarily be the same, or perhaps not even remotely similar, for all. We are assured that the plan of salvation provides for such tests and trials, but they are adapted to individual circumstances, capacities, and needs. President George Q. Cannon said:

> If we will be faithful to our God, He will redeem us, no matter what the circumstances may be through which we may be called to pass. We may wade through sorrow. We may have to endure persecution. We may have to meet with death. We may have to endure imprisonment and many other things that our predecessors had to endure. God may test us in this manner.
>
> Every human being that is connected with this work will have to be tested before he can enter into the Celestial Kingdom of our God. He will try us to the uttermost. If we have any spot more tender than another, He will feel after it. He will test all in some way or other.
>
> We have learned that there are plenty of trials and difficulties for all, if they will live faithful, to have their full share and all that are necessary to test them and their faith and integrity to the fullest extent. Each generation may not have to pass through exactly the same scenes. They are apt to vary as the circumstances which surround each vary; but they will, nevertheless, accomplish the desired end. There is one thing certain, every Latter-day Saint who is faithful to the truth and who lives to the or-

dinary age of man will have all the opportunities of this kind he or she can desire to gain experience and to have his or her zeal, integrity, courage and devotion to the truth fully exhibited. (*Gospel Truth,* pp. 301–2.)

Some people worry needlessly about such Abrahamic tests and wonder what the "big test" may be and when it may occur. Some even wonder if they are less than faithful because they have seemingly escaped the "big tests" of tragedy and tribulation. Others may speculate about whether the adversities they are presently experiencing constitute a personal Gethsemane that holds some special saving value. Such thoughts are fruitless and self-defeating. It appears that all we can know for sure is that God will indeed try us and our faith "to the uttermost" and that life's adversities are, at least in part, an important and essential element in that process. Furthermore, we may not be surprised by the testing nature of our trials and tribulations but may indeed be astonished by the fact that life's "big tests" are often much different than we expect. Elder Boyd K. Packer explained that there is an equality in this testing process, although each person's tests may drastically differ:

> The crucial test of life, I repeat, does not center in the choice between fame and obscurity, nor between wealth and poverty. The greatest decision of life is between good and evil.
>
> We may foolishly bring unhappiness and trouble, even suffering upon ourselves. These are not always to be regarded as penalties imposed by a displeased Creator. They are part of the lessons of life, part of the test.
>
> Some are tested by poor health, some by a body that is deformed or homely. Others are tested by handsome and healthy bodies; some by the passion of youth; others by the erosions of age.

Some suffer disappointment in marriage, family problems; others live in poverty and obscurity. Some (perhaps this is the hardest test) find ease and luxury.

All are part of the test, and there is more equality in this testing than sometimes we suspect. ("The Choice," p. 21.)

It is almost startling to hear or read these apostolic words. It may not be difficult to acknowledge that all will be tested "to the uttermost," as President Cannon said, but some of the tests identified by Elder Packer seem so attractive as to cause one to wonder wherein lies the testing. As difficult as it may be to understand and accept, some of life's greatest tests and trials may be associated with the comforts and conveniences that we so often desire and pursue. From scriptural precedent and prophetic commentary we learn that peace, pleasure, and prosperity are often more difficult tests and adversities than death, disease, and distress. President Ezra Taft Benson eloquently testified:

Every generation has its tests and its chance to stand and prove itself. Would you like to know of one of our toughest tests? Hear the warning words of President Brigham Young, "The worst fear I have about this people is that they will get rich in this country, forget God and His people, wax fat, and kick themselves out of the Church and go to hell. This people will stand mobbing, robbing, poverty and all manner of persecution and be true. But my greatest fear is that they cannot stand wealth."

Ours then seems to be the toughest test of all for the evils are more subtle, more clever. It all seems less menacing and it is harder to detect. While every test of righteousness represents a struggle, this particular test seems like no test at all, no struggle and so could be the most deceiving of all tests.

Do you know what peace and prosperity can do to a people—it can put them to sleep. The Book of Mormon warned us of how the devil, in the last days, would lead us away carefully down to hell.

The Lord has on the earth some potential spiritual giants whom He saved for some six thousand years to help bear off the Kingdom triumphantly and the devil is trying to put them to sleep. The devil knows that he probably won't be too successful in getting them to commit many great and malignant sins of commission. So he puts them into a deep sleep, like Gulliver, while he strands them with little sins of omission. And what good is a sleepy, neutralized, lukewarm giant as a leader?

We have too many potential spiritual giants who should be more vigorously lifting their homes, the kingdom, and the country. We have many who feel they are good men, but they need to be good for something—stronger patriarchs, courageous missionaries, valiant genealogists and temple workers, dedicated patriots, devoted quorum members. In short, we must be shaken and awakened from a spiritual snooze. (*Our Obligation and Challenge*, pp. 2-3.)

We need to recognize both the importance and the diversity of life's tests. Trials and tribulations may test our faith and integrity, but so may comfort and ease. Knowing that we "must needs be chastened and tried, even as Abraham" (D&C 101:4), to fulfill God's purposes for us and to be sanctified helps provide a general answer to the common queries, Why me? Why this? Why now? Whether by means of peace and prosperity or pain and problems, life is not only a time of testing but also a time of training.

Experience

Few, if any, of us have known the affliction and adversity that Joseph Smith encountered in his brief lifetime. In his anguish over the suffering of the Saints and over his own personal privation in Liberty Jail, he came to understand through revelation and personal experience the beneficial nature of life's many tribulations. In answer to his poignant pleas, the Lord extended comforting assurance to Joseph (and each of us) in one of the most beautiful and scripturally significant statements concerning the purpose for pain, tribulation, and suffering.

> If thou art called to pass through tribulation; if thou art in perils among false brethren; if thou art in perils among robbers; if thou art in perils by land or by sea;
>
> If thou art accused with all manner of false accusations; if thine enemies fall upon thee; if they tear thee from the society of thy father and mother and brethren and sisters; and if with a drawn sword thine enemies tear thee from the bosom of thy wife, and of thine offspring, and thine elder son, although but six years of age, shall cling to thy garments, and shall say, My father, my father, why can't you stay with us? O, my father, what are the men going to do with you? and if then he shall be thrust from thee by the sword, and thou be dragged to prison, and thine enemies prowl around thee like wolves for the blood of the lamb;
>
> And if thou shouldst be cast into the pit, or into the hands of murderers, and the sentence of death passed upon thee; if thou be cast into the deep; if the billowing surge conspire against thee; if fierce winds become thine enemy; if the heavens gather blackness, and all the elements combine to hedge up the way; and above all, if the very jaws of hell shall gape open the mouth wide after thee, know thou, my son, that all these things shall give thee experience, and shall be for thy good. (D&C 122:5–7.)

By the very nature of our existence and the purposes of the plan, each of us is enrolled in the "school of hard knocks." Adversity and affliction, regardless of the cause, provide us with a most necessary and unique tutorial. We cannot claim, when we become enveloped in the course curriculum and its difficult demands, that we are students in the school of suffering against our will. If the veil of forgetfulness could be parted momentarily, we would more profoundly perceive our enthusiastic acceptance and joyful anticipation of the opportunities and challenges of life on earth.

This education for eternity could be compared, to some extent, to earthly schooling. A student entering a university for the first time leaves home with a degree of apprehension and fear but thrills at the prospects such experiences will afford. He soon learns that there are challenging classes, stimulating assignments, and exciting experiments. There are fun times, friendships, and rewarding social experiences. But with it all will come those moments of discouragement—wondering if he can make it through another test or pressing assignment. There will also be boring classes, assignments that are difficult or monotonous, and times when the student wonders not only if he can make it another day but also if there is any "meaning in all the madness." All of these experiences, whether perceived as positive or negative, are essential in the educational experience and the enlargement of mind and character. Just as there could be no significant education at a university without intellectual and academic challenges that push students to their limits (and sometimes beyond), we cannot become enlarged and educated spiritually without the beneficial experience that results from adversity. Without tribulations and sorrows, life's core curriculum would be incomplete and totally inadequate. Orson F. Whitney taught:

> No pain that we suffer, no trial that we experience is wasted. It ministers to our education, to the development

of such qualities as patience, faith, fortitude and humility. All that we suffer and all that we endure, especially when we endure it patiently, builds up our characters, purifies our hearts, expands our souls, and makes us more tender and charitable, more worthy to be called the children of God . . . and it is through sorrow and suffering, toil and tribulation, that we gain the education that we come here to acquire and which will make us more like our Father and Mother in heaven. (As quoted by Elder Spencer W. Kimball in *Faith Precedes the Miracle,* pp. 98–99.)

The Lord's promise is that hardships—whatever their nature, whatever their cause—not only will give us experience but also will be for our good. Perhaps during those moments of pain and problems we may wonder how such suffering can actually be for our good. Benjamin Franklin characterized the beneficial nature of this kind of experience when he said, "Those things that hurt, instruct." It is a proven fact that we retain more from experiencing something than through merely hearing about it. When we are instructed in an unforgettably painful way, we remember and thus we grow. Truly the beneficial instruction of adversity and affliction, as President Joseph F. Smith said, "brings out our better natures." Just as opposition and adversity are for our good, absence of these experiences would deter our eternal progress. M. Scott Peck, a noted psychiatrist, author, and lecturer, has identified not only the positive nature of problems but also the negative side effects of the absence or avoidance of problems:

What makes life difficult is that the process of confronting and solving problems is a painful one. Problems, depending upon their nature, evoke in us frustration or grief or sadness or loneliness or guilt or regret or anger or fear or anxiety or anguish or despair. These are uncomfortable feelings, often very uncomfortable, often as painful as any kind of physical pain, sometimes equaling the very worst kind of physical pain. Indeed, it is *because* of the pain that events or conflicts engender in us that we call them problems. And since life poses an endless series of problems, life is always difficult and is full of pain as well as joy.

Yet it is in this whole process of meeting and solving problems that life has its meaning. Problems are the cutting edge that distinguishes between success and failure. Problems call forth our courage and our wisdom; indeed, they create our courage and our wisdom. It is only because of problems that we grow mentally and spiritually. When we desire to encourage the growth of the human spirit, we challenge and encourage the human capacity to solve problems, just as in school we deliberately set problems for our children to solve. It is through the pain of confronting and resolving problems that we learn. . . . It is for this reason that wise people learn not to dread but actually to welcome problems and actually to welcome the pain of problems.

Most of us are not so wise. Fearing the pain involved, almost all of us, to a greater or lesser degree, attempt to avoid problems. We procrastinate, hoping that they will go away. We ignore them, forget them, pretend they do not exist. We even take drugs to assist us in ignoring them, so that by deadening ourselves to the pain we can forget the problems that cause the pain. We attempt to skirt around problems rather than meet them head on. We attempt to get out of them rather than suffer through them.

This tendency to avoid problems and the emotional suffering inherent in them is the primary basis of all human mental illness. Since most of us have this tendency to a greater or lesser degree, most of us are mentally ill to a greater or lesser degree, lacking complete mental health. Some of us will go to quite extraordinary lengths to avoid our problems and the suffering they cause, proceeding far afield from all that is clearly good and sensible in order to

try to find an easy way out, building the most elaborate
fantasies in which to live, sometimes to the total exclusion
of reality. In the succinctly elegant words of Carl Jung,
"Neurosis is always a substitute for legitimate suffering."

But the substitute itself ultimately becomes more painful than the legitimate suffering it was designed to avoid.
. . . In any case, when we avoid the legitimate suffering
that results from dealing with problems, we also avoid the
growth that problems demand from us. (*The Road Less
Traveled*, pp. 16–17.)

The concepts taught by Peck in the previous statement
were illustrated in practical terms on a radio talk show that
I heard. The host of the show was a psychologist specializ-
ing in marriage and family therapy. She reported that in
her counseling she was encountering many parents whose
grown children were leaving good jobs to return home to
live with their parents. What was unusual about this situation was that these children, characterized as "yuppies,"
seemed to have everything going in their favor—good fami-
lies, good education, convenient and comfortable lives,
and prominent and prestigious occupations. But when
faced with challenges or frustrations, and feeling a void or
lack of fulfillment in life, these same successful children
"dropped out" and returned home to live.

Discussing this depressing dilemma with the parents,
the counselor discovered that each of the parents
characterized him or herself as a "child of the Great Depression." Each had had to struggle and work hard in life
to succeed and acquire material things. As parents they
vowed their children would never have to suffer and
scrape as they had done. As a result they indulged their
children and sought to make life for them as comfortable
and carefree as possible. These parents came to the stark
realization that what they did in order to make their children's lives easy was in fact one of the main reasons why

life was becoming so hard for them. The children now lacked the inner strength to face life's frustrations and set-backs. The parents had been successful later in life be-cause of their earlier battles with misfortune. Such ex-amples of success through struggle help us to see more clearly how "all these things shall give thee experience, and shall *be for thy good.*" Harold S. Kushner has pro-vided this insightful observation:

> Fun can be the dessert of our lives but never its main course. It can be a very welcome change of pace from the things we do every day, but should it ever become *what* we do every day, we will find it too frivolous a base to build a life on.
>
> I think of all the people I knew (and envied) in high school whose lives seemed to be so much more full of fun than mine—the athletes, the good-looking, smooth-talking students, the first ones to have serious boyfriends or girl-friends. We all envied them back then, because their lives seemed to be one long party, one fun experience after another. Neither they nor we could have known back then that a life of constant pleasure during those teenage years almost inevitably sets one up for a life of frustration after-ward. There are skills not acquired, habits not formed, and lessons about the real world not learned during those years of having everything go smoothly for you.
>
> . . . Will someone to whom things came effortlessly in youth ever learn the disciplines of patience and postponing gratification, or will that person be unprepared for the day when the music stops and people start saying no? (*When All You've Ever Wanted Isn't Enough,* pp. 69–70. Copy-right © 1986 by Kushner Enterprises, Inc. Reprinted by permission of Summit Books, a division of Simon & Schuster, Inc.)

Having a life of comfort, free from trials and tribula-tions and heartaches and hardships, may seem desirable to some but will actually leave us weak and empty. The discomforts of giving birth to a child may indeed be excruciatingly painful, but without that pain the joy that children can bring to parents' lives would not be as exquisite. Hoping to wrap ourselves in some sort of "security blanket" that would immunize us from pain and problems can actually rob us of some of life's greatest joys and most significant achievements. "God wants us to be stronger than we are—more fixed in our purpose, more certain of our commitments, eventually needing less coddling from him, showing more willingness to shoulder some of the burden of his heavy load," observed Jeffrey R. Holland. "In short, he wants us to be more like him." (*On Earth as it is in Heaven*, p. 162.) We, like an expectant mother in labor, must encounter our full share of pain and distress if we are to give birth to a new life—a new self with godlike strengths and capacities. That is the purpose and plan for such soul-stretching suffering and experience.

Experience gained in the crucible of adversity not only is for our own good and individual development but also is designed to further the works of God. President Hugh B. Brown often recited an insightful parable with autobiographical implications yet with universal application. "The Gardener and the Currant Bush" demonstrates how suffering that often seems cruel can not only be for our good but also promote the purposes of God and ripple with far-reaching possibilities.

> In the early dawn, a young gardener was pruning his trees and shrubs. He had one choice currant bush which had gone too much to wood. He feared therefore that it would produce little, if any, fruit.
>
> Accordingly, he trimmed and pruned the bush and cut it back. In fact, when he had finished, there was little left but stumps and roots.

Tenderly he considered what was left. It looked so sad and deeply hurt. On every stump there seemed to be a tear where the pruning knife had cut away the growth of early spring. The poor bush seemed to speak to him, and he thought he heard it say:

"Oh, how could you be so cruel to me; you who claim to be my friend, who planted me and cared for me when I was young, and nurtured and encouraged me to grow? Could you not see that I was rapidly responding to your care? I was nearly half as large as the trees across the fence, and might soon have become like one of them. But now you've cut my branches back; the green, attractive leaves are gone, and I am in disgrace among my fellows."

The young gardener looked at the weeping bush and heard its plea with sympathetic understanding. His voice was full of kindness as he said, "Do not cry; what I have done to you was necessary that you might be a prize currant bush in my garden. You were not intended to give shade or shelter by your branches. My purpose when I planted you was that you should bear fruit. When I want currants, a tree, regardless of its size, cannot supply the need.

"No, my little currant bush, if I had allowed you to continue to grow as you had started, all your strength would have gone to wood; your roots would not have gained a firm hold, and the purpose for which I brought you into my garden would have been defeated. Your place would have been taken by another, for you would have been barren. You must not weep; all this will be for your good; and some day, when you see more clearly, when you are richly laden with luscious fruit, you will thank me and say, 'Surely, he was a wise and loving gardener. He knew the purpose of my being, and I thank him now for what I then thought was cruelty.' "

Some years later, this young gardener was in a foreign land, and he himself was growing. He was proud of his position and ambitious for the future.

One day an unexpected vacancy entitled him to promotion. The goal to which he had aspired was now almost within his grasp, and he was proud of the rapid growth which he was making.

But for some reason unknown to him, another was appointed in his stead, and he was asked to take another post relatively unimportant and which, under the circumstances, caused his friends to feel that he had failed.

The young man staggered to his tent and knelt beside his cot and wept. He knew now that he could never hope to have what he had thought so desirable. He cried to God and said, "Oh, how could you be so cruel to me? You who claim to be my friend—you who brought me here and nurtured and encouraged me to grow. Could you not see that I was almost equal to the other men whom I have so long admired? But now I have been cut down. I am in disgrace among my fellows. Oh, how could you do this to me?"

He was humiliated and chagrined and a drop of bitterness was in his heart, when he seemed to hear an echo from the past. Where had he heard those words before? They seemed familiar. Memory whispered:

"I'm the gardener here."

He caught his breath. Ah, that was it—the currant bush! But why should that long-forgotten incident come to him in the midst of his hour of tragedy? And memory answered with words which he himself had spoken:

"Do not cry . . . what I have done to you was necessary . . . you were not intended for what you sought to be, . . . if I had allowed you to continue . . . you would have failed in the purpose for which I planted you and my plans for you would have been defeated. You must not weep; some day when you are richly laden with experience you will say, 'He was a wise gardener. He knew the purpose of my earth life. . . . I thank him now for what I thought was cruel.' "

His own words were the medium by which his prayer was answered. There was no bitterness in his heart as he humbly spoke again to God and said, "I know you now. *You* are the gardener, and *I* the currant bush. Help me, dear God, to endure the pruning, and to grow as you would have me grow; to take my allotted place in life and ever more to say, 'Thy will not mine be done.' " (*Eternal Quest*, pp. 243–45.)

Just as the gardener in President Brown's story told the currant bush that it was his design that the bush bear fruit, so God desires us to bear fruit. Our experiential sorrows and suffering yield a harvest not only in personal character development but also in furthering God's works through our subsequent compassionate service to others. Our individual pain and problems may not benefit others directly, but the traits we acquire and the experience we gain through that suffering can teach us how to serve and can enlarge our capacity to succor and strengthen others. Carl Jung once wisely observed, "Only the wounded doctor can heal." The scriptures and the lives of the Savior and his prophets testify of the power to bless and uplift that comes through suffering. The Apostle Paul, in the New Testament, and Alma, in the Book of Mormon, clearly taught that Jesus' compassion was influenced and shaped to a large degree by his own suffering:

Wherefore in all things it behoved him to be made like unto his brethren, that he might be a merciful and faithful high priest in things pertaining to God, to make reconciliation for the sins of the people.

For in that he himself hath suffered being [tried], he is able to succour them that are [tried]. (Hebrews 2:17–18.)

> And he shall go forth, suffering pains and afflictions and temptations of every kind; and this that the word might be fulfilled which saith he will take upon him the pains and the sicknesses of his people.
>
> And he will take upon him death, that he may loose the bands of death which bind his people; and he will take upon him their infirmities, that his bowels may be filled with mercy, according to the flesh, that he may know according to the flesh how to succor his people according to their infirmities. (Alma 7:11–12.)

Through his grueling ordeals Joseph Smith was likewise tutored and trained in empathy, compassion, and service. From his suffering in his cell in Liberty Jail he wrote: "Those who have not been enclosed in the walls of prison without cause or provocation, can have but little idea how sweet the voice of a friend is; one token of friendship from any source whatever awakens and calls into action every sympathetic feeling . . . until finally all enmity, malice and hatred, and past differences, misunderstandings and mismanagements are slain victorious at the feet of hope" (*History of the Church* 3:293).

The experience obtained through affliction is purposeful—designed for the development of Christlike qualities in the individual. But for these acquired qualities to become truly Christlike they must be channeled to the healing and helping of others. President Joseph F. Smith referred to this ultimate experience and good gained from adversity when he taught, as mentioned previously, that such was designed to "quicken [our] devotion to others." It is through service that those inner strengths and Christlike capacities are demonstrated, ratified, and refined. Paradoxically, finding one's life, as the Savior taught, comes only through the giving of one's life in selfless service to others (see Matthew 10:39).

When we grapple with our own trials and tribulations, whatever their cause, we will naturally become introspective, asking ourselves questions such as: Why is this happening? How can this be for my own good? What beneficial experience can possibly come from this terrible tragedy? The answers to these questions may not be readily apparent, but they may come more clearly into view when we ask and act upon the more relevant question, How can I now help others who may be suffering in similar ways? Often the afflictions and adversities that we suffer in life, though deeply personal, are not unique to us. All around us there are people who suffer in similar ways, people who can benefit from our experience and the good we have gained. The mother who has lost a child to an untimely death can provide solace and support to another grieving parent in a way that perhaps no other could. A person who has been ostracized and knows the depths of loneliness can, in a more sensitive and sincere manner than one who has always been with the ''in crowd,'' extend friendship and fellowship to others who have been left out. In addition one need not suffer in the same way as another in order to empathize with and strengthen him. Rabbi Kushner describes how the experience of affliction enabled one man to provide a unique and valuable service:

> Many years ago, when I was young, a business associate of my father's died under particularly tragic circumstances, and I accompanied my father to the funeral. The man's widow and children were surrounded by clergy and psychiatrists trying to ease their grief and make them feel better. They knew all the right words, but nothing helped. They were beyond being comforted. The widow kept saying, ''You're right, I know you're right, but it doesn't make any difference.'' Then a man walked in, a big burly man in his eighties who was a legend in the toy

and game industry. He had escaped from Russia as a youth after having been arrested and tortured by the czar's secret police. He had come to this country illiterate and penniless and had built up an immensely successful company. He was known as a hard bargainer, a ruthless competitor. Despite his success, he had never learned to read or write. He hired people to read his mail to him. The joke in the industry was that he could write a check for a million dollars, and the hardest part would be signing his name at the bottom. He had been sick recently, and his face and his walking showed it. But he walked over to the widow and started to cry, and she cried with him, and you could feel the atmosphere in the room change. This man who had never read a book in his life spoke the language of the heart and held the key that opened the gates of solace where learned doctors and clergy could not. (*When All You've Ever Wanted Isn't Enough,* pp. 109–10. See copyright and permission information, p. 69 herein.)

The challenges we face in life that so often and so poignantly tug at our tender heartstrings are purposely designed by our loving Father to bless and benefit us as we "mourn with those that mourn . . . and comfort those that stand in need of comfort" (Mosiah 18:9). I have come to know the value of adversity in expanding our capacity to serve. In my own life there have been dark days when I could discern little purpose for my suffering. There have been moments of discouragement and distress when I questioned the Lord's purposes as well as my ability to endure another day. There have been testing and trying, though my afflictions may seem puny in comparison to those of Abraham, Job, Joseph Smith, and thousands of others who have suffered much more than I have. Yet my pains and problems were very real to me. In retrospect I see more clearly how my most difficult and disquieting moments were training and shaping me to later serve as a bishop and help others who were facing many of the same dilemmas and difficulties that I had encountered. How thankful I am now for those adversities, as hurtful and annoying as they were at the time, for they empowered me to experience the Christlike joy of lifting the burdens of others, and from them eventually came as much pleasure as pain. Did God allow these adversities to come into my life in order to prepare me for a Church calling? I do not know, but I can testify from profound personal experience that—whatever the cause, whatever the purpose, whatever the relationship to the plan of salvation—they were for my good, essential for my experience, and influential in my service.

There are many things that I cannot fully see with my earthly eyes or understand with my mortal mind, but I with Nephi declare, "Nevertheless, I know in whom I have trusted. . . . Rejoice, O my heart, and cry unto the Lord, and say: O Lord, I will praise thee forever; yea, my soul will rejoice in thee, my God, and the rock of my salvation." (2 Nephi 4:19, 30.)

CHAPTER FOUR

Strength to Endure

Each of us, through the natural journey of life and in fulfillment of the plan of salvation, will face many obstacles and "much tribulation." Our response to suffering, rather than the particular type of suffering, seems to dictate whether adversity makes us *bitter* or *better*. Some become spiritually broken and emotionally disabled through disappointment and difficulties. Others come through similar testing experiences refined and strengthened. Some endure excruciatingly painful and torturous circumstances and come forth spiritually stronger, more sensitive and compassionate, firmer in faith. Yet others who may suffer significantly less may become embittered and unhappy with life and, with cankered souls, blame God for their woes and turn from religion. Even among the members of the same family, two or more people may face the same afflictions, yet their responses to that adversity may be poles apart. This diversity of responses to the same adversity is represented in the following true story from early Church history recounted by Elder Jack H. Goaslind:

> Over one hundred years ago a Swedish family who had joined the Church faced a long ocean voyage to America, a train trip from New York to Omaha, and then a trek by wagon train to Salt Lake City. During their train trip they rode in stock cars used to haul hogs. The cars were filthy and filled with hog lice. On their wagon trip across the plains, a healthy baby was born, but their three-year-old contracted cholera. During the night, the father went to a neighboring wagon to borrow a candle, but was told they couldn't spare one. This angered him, and he fumed as he sat in the dark with his son's limp, feverish body in his arms. The boy died that night.
>
> The next morning the wagon master said they would hold a short funeral and bury the boy in a shallow grave. They were in Indian country and didn't have time to do more. The father insisted on staying behind and digging a grave deep enough so the animals would not disturb the body. They experienced other hardships before they reached Salt Lake City.
>
> Now, both the mother and the father experienced the same trials, but the father became withdrawn, cantankerous, and bitter. He stopped going to church, found fault with Church leaders. He became caught up in his own miseries, and the light of Christ grew dimmer and dimmer in his life.
>
> On the other hand, the mother's faith increased. Each new problem seemed to make her stronger. She became an angel of mercy—filled with empathy, compassion, and charity. She was a light to those around her. Her family gravitated toward her and looked to her as their leader. She was happy; he was miserable. ("Happiness," p. 54.)

Amidst our afflictions, usually when we ask questions such as, Why is this happening to me? we are not really seeking for cognitive answers to mortally unanswerable questions. Instead, through those questions, we are summoning spiritual strength and pleading for power to be able to endure. Knowing the answers may not necessarily add to our capacity to endure. The scriptures speak of the exalting power that comes from enduring adversity rather than merely understanding it. To the Prophet Joseph, the Lord declared, "My son, peace be unto thy soul; thine adversity and thine afflictions shall be but a small moment; and then, if thou endure it well, God shall exalt thee on high" (D&C 121:7–8).

In our own day modern Apostles not only have taught the need to endure well but also have distinguished between the celestial trait of "patient endurance" and the attitude of merely "putting up with" life's adversities. "Patient endurance is to be distinguished from merely being 'acted upon,' " declared Elder Neal A. Maxwell. "Endurance is more than pacing up and down within the cell of our circumstance; it is not only acceptance of things allotted to us, but to 'act for ourselves' by magnifying what is allotted to us (Alma 29:3, 6). . . . True enduring represents not merely the passage of time, but the passage of the soul." (" 'Endure It Well,' " pp. 33–34.) Elder Marvin J. Ashton has taught that personal greatness and depth of discipleship are determined to a large degree by how we respond to and endure the adversities of life:

Sometimes the most challenging form of endurance is found in trying to stay with our priorities, commitments, and assignments. How easy it is for some of us to lose our way when the unexpected, and seemingly undeserved, surface in our lives. Greatness is best measured by how well an individual responds to the happenings in life that appear to be totally unfair, unreasonable, and undeserved. Sometimes we are inclined to put up with a situation rather than endure. To endure is to bear up under, to stand firm against, to suffer without yielding, to continue to be, or to exhibit the state or power of lasting. . . .

When heartaches, tragedies, disappointments, injury, unusual attention, fame, or excessive prosperity become part of our lives, our challenges and responsibilities will be to endure them well. God will assist us in our quest to conquer, triumph, and continue if we humbly rededicate ourselves to the meaningful declaration "We have endured many things, and hope to be able to endure all things" (Articles of Faith 1:13). (" 'If Thou Endure It Well,' " p. 22.)

What makes the difference in whether a person merely "puts up with" adversity or truly endures — "stands firm against" — life's storms of suffering? The qualities of character necessary to endure are primarily spiritual qualities that come only from turning to God — through soliciting his support and seeking his strength. Each of us needs to come to realize that, as Rabbi Harold Kushner observed, " 'Why did this happen to me?' is not a question, but a cry of pain." He goes on to give the following counsel: "The best advice I can give is that the longer you focus on 'Why?' the more helpless you feel. There's nothing you can do to change the why, so I urge people to turn around and instead ask, 'What do I do now, and where do I find the strength, grace and courage to get over this and go on with my life?' I believe those abilities come primarily from God. God doesn't send us the problems, the sickness, the accident — He sends us the personal qualities to survive the tragedy." (In Ellen Byron, comp., " 'The Best Advice I Can Give You,' " p. 68.)

The scriptures and the inspired words of living prophets are the primary channels through which God sends us the spiritual strength to not only survive but also triumph in tribulation. Following are ten scriptural suggestions that have specific relevance to the enduring of times of trouble and tribulation. As we strive to apply these scriptural teachings we will see our spiritual strength increased and our capacity to endure enhanced. It is this spiritual strength, acquired through spiritual means, that enlarges us as individuals, enabling us not only to better endure but also to better serve and strengthen others. Gaining such spiritual strength is the vital difference between faithfully enduring adversity, as the Lord desires of us, and merely coping with it.

"Though He Slay Me, Yet Will I Trust in Him"

President Joseph F. Smith taught, "It is not easy for men to give up their vanities, to overcome their preconceived notions, and surrender themselves heart and soul to the will of God which is always higher than their own" (*Gospel Doctrine,* p. 9). Because of this natural tendency of men to, as Joseph Smith said, "walk in their own paths as they are pointed out by their own fingers" (see *Teachings of the Prophet Joseph Smith,* p. 26), perhaps the most difficult words for us to say (and really mean) during times of adversity are, "Thy will be done." The recurring reluctance of mere mortals to totally trust God and to surrender themselves to his will is a problem of perspective. We often acknowledge with our *heads* that God's ways are higher than our ways (see Isaiah 55:8-9), but when faced with the inherent ironies and seeming inequities of adversity, we may sometimes feel in our *hearts* that God doesn't know what he's doing and that there is no "meaning in all the madness." When God's will and

designs painfully collide with our own idea of what is best
for us, we often resist and resent his efforts because we do
not perceive his purposes. Elder James E. Talmage profoundly taught this principle by using an insightful personal experience:

> Sometimes I find myself under obligations of work re-
> quiring quiet and seclusion such as neither my comfort-
> able office nor the cozy study at home insures. My
> favorite retreat is an upper room in the tower of a large
> building, well removed from the noise and confusion of
> the city streets. The room is somewhat difficult of access,
> and relatively secure against human intrusion. Therein I
> have spent many peaceful and busy hours with books and
> pen.
>
> I am not always without visitors, however, especially in
> summertime; for, when I sit with windows open, flying in-
> sects occasionally find entrance and share the place with
> me. These self-invited guests are not unwelcome. Many a
> time I have laid down the pen, and, forgetful of my
> theme, have watched with interest the activities of these
> winged visitants, with an after-thought that the time so
> spent had not been wasted, for, is it not true, that even a
> butterfly, a beetle, or a bee, may be a bearer of lessons to
> the receptive student?
>
> A wild bee from the neighboring hills once flew into
> the room; and at intervals during an hour or more I
> caught the pleasing hum of its flight. The little creature re-
> alized that it was a prisoner, yet all its efforts to find the
> exit through the partly opened casement failed. When
> ready to close up the room and leave, I threw the window
> wide, and tried at first to guide and then to drive the bee
> to liberty and safety, knowing well that if left in the room
> it would die as other insects there entrapped had perished
> in the dry atmosphere of the enclosure. The more I tried
> to drive it out, the more determinedly did it oppose and
> resist my efforts. Its erstwhile peaceful hum developed

into an angry roar; its darting flight became hostile and threatening.

Then it caught me off my guard and stung my hand—the hand that would have guided it to freedom. At last it alighted on a pendant attached to the ceiling, beyond my reach of help or injury. The sharp pain of its unkind sting aroused in me rather pity than anger. I knew the inevitable penalty of its mistaken opposition and defiance; and I had to leave the creature to its fate. Three days later I returned to the room and found the dried, lifeless body of the bee on the writing table. It had paid for its stubbornness with its life.

To the bee's short-sightedness and selfish misunderstanding I was a foe, a persistent persecutor, a mortal enemy bent on its destruction; while in truth I was its friend, offering it ransom of the life it had put in forfeit through its own error, striving to redeem it, in spite of itself, from the prison-house of death and restore it to the outer air of liberty.

Are we so much wiser than the bee that no analogy lies between its unwise course and our lives? We are prone to contend, sometimes with vehemence and anger, against the adversity which after all may be the manifestation of superior wisdom and loving care, directed against our temporary comfort for our permanent blessing. In the tribulations and sufferings of mortality there is a divine ministry which only the godless soul can wholly fail to discern. To many the loss of wealth has been a boon, a providential means of leading or driving them from the confines of selfish indulgence to the sunshine and open, where boundless opportunity waits on effort. Disappointment, sorrow, and affliction may be the expression of an all-wise Father's kindness.

Consider the lesson of the unwise bee!

"Trust in the Lord with all thine heart; and lean not unto thine own understanding. In all thy ways acknowledge him, and he shall direct thy paths." (Proverbs 3:5-6.) ("The Parable of the Unwise Bee," pp. 1008-9.)

Like the unwise bee, we often resist and rebel against the afflictions and adversities of life because with our mortal, finite perspective we misinterpret the designs of God. With increased understanding of eternal principles and purposes, our perspective of the perplexities of this life is also altered and expanded. Through the revealed answers to life's important questions—Where did I come from? Why am I here on earth? Where am I going when I die?—we can better perceive the divine objective for adversity and affliction in mortality. The gospel does not provide, at least in this life, all of the answers, but it does provide enough perspective to help us endure. Understanding the doctrinal implications of the "there and then," as Elder Neal A. Maxwell has observed, helps us better understand and endure the challenges of the "here and now."

> Premortality, mortality, and postmortality have been compared to a three-act play, of which we are witnessing the second act. Not having seen (remembered) the first act, we have to rely on reports from those who have received revelation. Those who are without these reports have inadequate knowledge concerning the preceding "there and then," and hence the injustice and unevenness of the "here and now" have caused some to call God's justice into question along with His capacity to achieve His purposes.
>
> Without an understanding of premortality, it is no wonder that mortals often fail to take account of what is perhaps mortality's most prominent feature—its stern proving and tutoring dimensions. Some then use life's trials as an argument against God, instead of accepting these trials as being something "common to man," or as the needed tutorials which, though rigorous, last "but for a small moment" (1 Corinthians 10:13; D&C 122:4). . . .
>
> With the acceptance of knowledge about premortality [and other important doctrines of the plan of salvation]

comes a greater realization of what it means to be true to ourselves and our possibilities. We can even understand better the role of life's disappointments and of opposition, the full shock of which we still feel, despite that understanding, but now within the absorptive framework of faith. (*A Wonderful Flood of Light*, pp. 38, 46.)

In contrast to the unwise bee who, lacking the broader perspective, misinterpreted and rebelled against the efforts to liberate him, Job trusted and submitted to God even when his own wife urged him to "curse God, and die" (Job 2:9). The breadth and depth of Job's afflictions almost surpass comprehension. His friends and family could not understand God's purposes for Job, although they offered their unsolicited and disconcerting ideas as to why Job suffered so. The scriptural account gives no evidence that Job fully understood, cognitively or spiritually, why he was being subjected to such misery. In fact his poignant pleadings with the Lord seem to indicate that he, too, was at a loss for a logical explanation. Despite all this, Job stands as an example of endurance. "Though he slay me," he declared, "yet will I trust in him" (Job 13:15).

The scriptures and modern prophets beckon us to follow the exemplary footsteps of Job. Our willingness to trust when we don't understand and to exercise faith when we feel forsaken is an imperative ingredient in our mortal "survival kit" that enables us to endure life's inexplicable inequities. "God is our refuge and strength, a very present help in trouble," sang the Psalmist in a poetic testimony of the power of trusting in the Lord.

> Therefore will not we fear, though the earth be removed, and though the mountains be carried into the midst of the sea;
> Though the waters thereof roar and be troubled, though the mountains shake with the swelling thereof. . . .

There is a river, the streams whereof shall make glad the city of God, the holy place of the tabernacles of the most High.

God is in the midst of her; she shall not be moved; God shall help her, and that right early.

The heathen raged, the kingdoms were moved: he uttered his voice, the earth melted.

The Lord of hosts is with us; the God of Jacob is our refuge. . . .

Be still, and know that I am God: I will be exalted among the heathen, I will be exalted in the earth.

The Lord of hosts is with us; the God of Jacob is our refuge. (Psalm 46:1–7, 10–11.)

Numerous scriptural passages declare the absolute necessity of trusting in God, not only in times of trouble, but in all our mortal endeavors (see Isaiah 50:10; Mosiah 4:6; Mormon 9:20; D&C 11:12–13). The benefits of an abiding trust in God far surpass a mere bestowal of strength to endure mortal hardships. Submission to God and trusting in his purposes have soul-saving power and are essential to exaltation. Alma declared to his son Helaman that "whosoever shall put their trust in God shall be supported in their trials, and their troubles, and their afflictions, and shall be lifted up at the last day" (Alma 36:3; see also Alma 38:5). Likewise, in our day President Ezra Taft Benson has testified of the comfort that comes from trusting God and of the power of salvation that accompanies this trust:

Let not your faith waver. God still rules. He is at the helm. He has not forgotten you, nor will He do so, if you keep sacred your covenants as members of His Church. And if the clouds gather for a moment, be assured that behind every cloud for you there is a smiling providence. "What though the clouds seem dark today? / Tomorrow's will be blue. / When every cloud has cleared away, / God's Providence shines through."

It is a great blessing to have an inner peace, to have an assurance, to have a spirit of serenity and inward calm during times of strife and struggle, during times of sorrow and reverses. It is soul-satisfying to know that God is at the helm, that He is mindful of His children, and that we can with full confidence place our trust in Him.

There is no place for fear among men and women who place their trust in the Almighty, who do not hesitate to humble themselves in seeking divine guidance through prayer. Though persecutions arise, though reverses come, in prayer we can find reassurance, for God will speak peace to the soul. That peace, that spirit of serenity, is a great blessing. (*Teachings of Ezra Taft Benson*, pp. 68-69.)

Enhanced endurance of life's adversities results only from our willingness to trust God even when hearts may be breaking and understanding may be absent. Without this assurance—that God loves us, that he is mindful of our needs, and that he is working a work that will enlarge us and exalt us—all other efforts to find peace for our troubled souls and strength to endure tribulation will be limited. The efficacy of prayer, scripture study, church service, and other such endeavors hinges, to a large degree, on our willingness to "walk to the edge of the light." This is illustrated in the following account by Elder Boyd K. Packer:

Some years ago I learned a lesson that I shall never forget.

I had been called as an Assistant to the Council of the Twelve, and we were to move to Salt Lake City and find an adequate and permanent home. President Henry D. Moyle assigned someone to help us.

A home was located that was ideally suited to our needs. Elder Harold B. Lee came and looked it over very carefully and then counseled, "By all means, you are to proceed."

But there was no way we could proceed. I had just completed the course work on a doctor's degree and was writing the dissertation. With the support of my wife and our eight children, all of the resources we could gather over the years had been spent on education.

By borrowing on our insurance, gathering every resource, we could barely get into the house, without sufficient left to even make the first monthly payment.

Brother Lee insisted, "Go ahead. I know it is right."

I was in deep turmoil because I had been counseled to do something I had never done before—to sign a contract without having the resources to meet the payments.

When Brother Lee sensed my feelings he sent me to President David O. McKay, who listened very carefully as I explained the circumstances.

He said, "You do this. It is the right thing." But he extended no resources to make the doing of it possible.

When I reported to Brother Lee he said, "That confirms what I have told you."

I was still not at peace, and then came the lesson. Elder Lee said, "Do you know what is wrong with you —you always want to see the end from the beginning."

I replied quietly that I wanted to see at least a few steps ahead. He answered by quoting from the sixth verse of the twelfth chapter of Ether: "Wherefore, dispute not because ye see not, for ye receive no witness until after the trial of your faith."

And then he added, "My boy, you must learn to walk to the edge of the light, and perhaps a few steps into the darkness, and you will find that the light will appear and move ahead of you."

And so it has—but only as we walked to the edge of the light. (*The Holy Temple*, pp. 183–85.)

Trusting in the Lord in times of sorrow and suffering requires us not only to walk to "the edge of the light" but also, when compelled by our circumstances, to walk on in the dark paths of uncertainty. Only when we are willing to put total trust in the "Light of the World" will the darkness be dispelled and the pathway of endurance and spiritual strength become illuminated. Just as the Lord reassured the early Saints during a dark time of trouble and persecution, so he extends to us his beckoning invitation to trust in him and in his promise of comfort: "Let your hearts be comforted . . . for all flesh is in mine hands; be still and know that I am God" (D&C 101:16).

"Pray Always, and I Will Pour Out My Spirit upon You"

The Apostle James declared, "The effectual fervent prayer of a righteous man availeth much" (James 5:16). This scriptural promise holds monumental meaning in our times of adversity. Amidst pain and problems our souls inherently yearn for divine comfort. Our prayerful pleadings will not go unheard. The Lord himself has promised us relief and comfort in our tribulations if we will "pray always, and not faint" (2 Nephi 32:9; see also D&C 88:126; Luke 18:1). Jeremiah prophesied to the Jews in Jerusalem that, despite their impending bondage and the tribulations that would accompany that seventy-year captivity, the Lord would hearken to their faithful pleadings:

> For thus saith the Lord, That after seventy years be accomplished at Babylon I will visit you, and perform my good word toward you, in causing you to return to this place.

For I know the thoughts that I think toward you, saith the Lord, thoughts of peace, and not of evil, to give you an expected end.

Then shall ye call upon me, and ye shall go and pray unto me, and I will hearken unto you.

And ye shall seek me, and find me, when ye shall search for me with all your heart.

And I will be found of you, saith the Lord: and I will turn away your captivity, and I will gather you from all the nations, and from all the places whither I have driven you, saith the Lord; and I will bring you again into the place whence I caused you to be carried away captive. (Jeremiah 29:10–14.)

This ancient prophetic promise concerning the redemption and gathering of the Jews and their return to Jerusalem also confirms to us the Lord's modern promise to similarly reclaim us from the captivity of our own individual adversities and restore to our souls peace and security. An account in the Book of Mormon dramatically portrays and testifies of the strengthening power of personal prayer in times of tribulation. After Alma and his followers fled from King Noah and his wicked priests, they established the Church and prospered spiritually as they faithfully lived the gospel in the land of Helam. Their peace and comfort were shattered, however, when they were captured and enslaved by the Lamanites. They were ultimately subjected to the harsh rule of Amulon, formerly one of the wicked priests in King Noah's court, who was now in alliance with the Lamanites. As slaves to the Lamanites, Alma's people were forced to be "beasts of burden." Under their heavy burdens, both physical and emotional, Alma's people cried unto the Lord for relief from their afflictions.

And it came to pass that so great were their afflictions that they began to cry mightily to God.

And Amulon commanded them that they should stop their cries; and he put guards over them to watch them, that whosoever should be found calling upon God should be put to death.

And Alma and his people did not raise their voices to the Lord their God, but did pour out their hearts to him; and he did know the thoughts of their hearts.

And it came to pass that the voice of the Lord came to them in their afflictions, saying: Lift up your heads and be of good comfort, for I know of the covenant which ye have made unto me; and I will covenant with my people and deliver them out of bondage.

And I will also ease the burdens which are put upon your shoulders, that even you cannot feel them upon your backs, even while you are in bondage; and this will I do that ye may stand as witnesses for me hereafter, and that ye may know of a surety that I, the Lord God, do visit my people in their afflictions.

And now it came to pass that the burdens which were laid upon Alma and his brethren were made light; yea, the Lord did strengthen them that they could bear up their burdens with ease, and they did submit cheerfully and with patience to all the will of the Lord. (Mosiah 24:10–15.)

Implicit in this testimony of God's faithfulness to his promise to "visit [his] people in their afflictions" is the message that he usually answers our prayers not by lifting the burdens and tribulations but rather by bolstering our capacity to endure them. Not too infrequently, and quite naturally, we may become discouraged that our problems and pains persist despite prolonged prayerfulness. In these perplexing moments it becomes easy to let faith waver, to second guess God's purposes, or even to feel that the Lord is disregarding our prayerful petitions and pleadings before him. The truth of the matter may very well be, as evidenced by Alma's account, that the Lord often answers our prayers and provides comfort in a different manner

than we desire or expect. Kay Yow, coach of the 1988 U.S.
Women's Olympic basketball team, tells how the Lord
answered her prayers when she was diagnosed as having
breast and lymphatic cancer: "My immediate tendency
was to pray to God that this circumstance might change.
But in my case it didn't happen. *God chose to change me
instead of my circumstance,* and through the whole experience I have grown deeply. I'm a better person in a lot of
ways." (*USA Today,* 22 October 1987, p. 10C; italics
added.)

The Lord has assured us that he is not far from us, that
our prayers are indeed heard, and that he will come to our
aid in our times of trouble. If we do not avail ourselves,
through fervent prayer, of this promised relief, we may
sadly discover that our souls become spiritually brittle and
easily broken by the whirlwinds of adversity. "There
seems to be a reason why we lose our composure in adversity – why we think we can no longer cope with what we're
faced with here in this life," observed Bishop H. Burke
Peterson.

> There is a reason why we give up, why we "fall apart at
> the seams," so to speak. The reason may be so simple
> that we lose sight of it.
> Could it be because we begin to lose contact with our
> greatest source of strength – our Father in heaven? He is
> the key to our enjoying sweetness in adversity – in gaining
> strength from our trials – he and he alone. . . .
> . . . We will have no temptation or trial beyond our
> ability to overcome. He will provide a way for us to rise
> above whatever the trial may be.
> May I suggest that the best way I know to keep close
> to the source of this great strength is through prayer. No
> man can stand alone in his struggle through life. Some-
> times in discouragement our prayers, at best, become oc-
> casional or maybe not at all. Sometimes we forget or just
> don't care. . . .

Sincere prayer is the heart of a happy and productive life. Prayer strengthens faith. Prayer is the preparation for miracles. . . .

As we learn to develop this two-way communication, the standard of our life will improve. We will see things more clearly; we will try harder to do better; we will see the real joy that can come through trials and testing. Although problems will still be with us, peace, contentment, and true happiness will be ours in abundance. . . .

Yes, the trials will still be there; but with the companionship of the Spirit, our approach to trials will change frustrations and heartaches to blessings. ("Adversity and Prayer," pp. 107–8.)

The scriptures clearly and emphatically remind us that there is indeed a soul-strengthening power flowing from fervent prayer. It is important, however, to note a significant scriptural addendum to the charge to "cry unto the Lord." Many scriptural passages add the important word *always*, or other similar words, to this divine injunction.

Men ought *always* to pray, and not to faint (Luke 18:1).

Pray *without ceasing* (1 Thessalonians 5:17).

We will give ourselves *continually* to prayer (Acts 6:4).

Rejoicing in hope; patient in tribulation; *continuing instant* [constantly persisting] in prayer (Romans 12:12).

Yea, humble yourselves, and *continue* in prayer unto him. . . .

Cry unto him in your houses, yea, over all your household, *both morning, mid-day, and evening.* . . .

Yea, and when you do not cry unto the Lord, let your hearts be full, drawn out in prayer unto him *continually* for your welfare. (Alma 34:19, 21, 27.)

Pray always, that you may come off conqueror (D&C 10:5).

Pray always, and I will pour out my Spirit upon you,
and great shall be your blessing (D&C 19:38).

From these and numerous other passages we see that
the Lord desires *continual* faith and prayerfulness rather
than sporadic spiritual pleadings amidst our anguish and
adversity. Fervency without frequency does not yield the
same spiritual strength in times of adversity as do con-
stancy and consistency coupled with faith and feeling. The
Lord chided those who only come unto him in times of
trouble—those who, because of grievous ordeals, now fer-
vently seek him, but who previously in prosperity lacked
frequency in faith, diligence, and prayerfulness. "I, the
Lord, have suffered the affliction to come upon them,
wherewith they have been afflicted, in consequence of
their transgressions. . . . They were slow to hearken unto
the voice of the Lord their God; therefore, the Lord their
God is slow to hearken unto their prayers, to answer them
in the day of their trouble. In the day of their peace they es-
teemed lightly my counsel; but, in the day of their trouble,
of necessity they feel after me." (D&C 101:2, 7–8.)

Prayerfulness in times of adversity is important in gaining spiritual strength, but continual, ardent prayerfulness,
even in times of ease and comfort, is perhaps more critical
to faithful endurance. It may be that the most important
and most endurance-enhancing prayers we offer will not
be those tender pleadings we utter in our sorrow and suffering, but those simple, frequent prayers offered each day
of our lives. Our capacity to endure is being continually
shaped—by each faith-filled prayer. In addition to helping
us resist Satan's temptations, the Lord's counsel to "pray
always, that you may come off conqueror," seems also to
apply to conquering the potentially devastating effects of
adversity. Such effects are conquered through continual
struggles rather than by one brief, frantic skirmish. Elder
Howard W. Hunter observed:

We will all have some adversity in our lives. I think we can be reasonably sure of that. Some of it will have the potential to be violent and damaging and destructive. Some of it may even strain our faith in a loving God who has the power to administer relief in our behalf.

To those anxieties I think the Father of us all would say, "Why are ye so fearful? how is it that ye have no faith?" And of course that has to be faith for the whole journey, the entire experience, the fulness of our life, not simply around the bits and pieces and tempestuous moments. At the end of the journey, an end none of us can see now, we will say, "Master, the terror is over. . . . Linger, Oh, blessed Redeemer! Leave me alone no more." ("'Master, the Tempest Is Raging,'" pp. 34–35.)

The prophet Jacob's promise to his people concerning the blessing of prayer in times of their trials stands as a powerful prophetic promise to us today as we face our own challenges: "Look unto God with firmness of mind, and pray unto him with exceeding faith, and he will console you in your afflictions" (Jacob 3:1).

"All Things Shall Work Together for Good to Them That Walk Uprightly"

Fervent, faithful, and frequent prayers are essential for enhanced endurance of life's vicissitudes, but unless such prayers are accompanied by works of righteousness they are "vain, and availeth you nothing" (Alma 34:28; see also James 2:14–16). Obedience to the commandments of God and faithfulness to covenants taken are imperative in gaining the spiritual strength needed to faithfully endure and prosper amidst mortality's hardships and heartaches. The Lord promised the ancient Israelites that they would be blessed and prospered if they would be obedient to his laws and commandments (see Deuteronomy 28:1–14). To the Nephites he reiterated the relationship between obedience and the promised blessings of peace and prosperity: "Inasmuch as those whom the Lord God shall bring out of the land of Jerusalem shall keep his commandments, they shall prosper upon the face of this land. . . . And if it so be that they shall keep his commandments they shall be blessed upon the face of this land, and there shall be none to molest them, nor to take away the land of their inheritance; and they shall dwell safely forever." (2 Nephi 1:9.)

Numerous other scriptural passages add their confirming witnesses that walking uprightly before the Lord yields blessings of peace, prosperity, comfort, and happiness. In this dispensation we have received this promise of the Lord: "Therefore, let your hearts be comforted; for all things shall work together for good to them that walk uprightly" (D&C 100:15). Such prophetic promises may seem hollow at times when we have diligently kept the commandments yet face enormous challenges and tribulations. In these moments we must remember that walking uprightly before the Lord in obedience to his commandments will not *isolate* us from all of life's adversities, but such faithfulness can and will indeed *insulate* us with an increased endurance capacity. Likewise we must acknowledge that the promised "prosperity" may be much different than we expect. Alan Webster gives us the following insight concerning this idea:

> Perhaps the problem lies in our tendency to think of prosperity only as it is represented by material wealth or lack of serious problems. The word *prosperity* itself comes from the Latin *pro + spes*, which means "hope." Though the word soon came to mean "succeed" and is often used in the sense of material success, it does *not* necessarily mean an abundance of temporal possessions—or even a relatively comfortable, problem-free life. . . .

The truly righteous *are* prosperous, in the sense that they have confidence, which triggers faith into activity and creates beneficial circumstances from less-favorable ones. They do not wait for the Lord to give or withhold rewards, but instead call on him for guidance about what will be most beneficial for them, both temporally and spiritually. (In *Ensign,* April 1990, pp. 52–53.)

Although we will not be completely free from trials and tribulations, through keeping the commandments we can, with increased confidence, call upon the Lord for additional strength and spiritual guidance. Like the blessings of prayer, the soul-strengthening power resulting from obedience to gospel principles is more effectively increased through *cumulative righteousness* than through crisis-induced faithfulness or "deathbed repentance." Just as reservoirs collect the life-giving waters of the spring runoff and dispense the necessary moisture during the most critical times, we are constantly collecting spiritual strength that will help see us through periods of dearth and deprivation in our lives. If the watermasters were vigilant in their task only in times of severe drought, disaster would inevitably result from the lack of water held in reserve. In a similar vein, every act of obedience adds to our "spiritual reservoirs" of strength and endurance. Elder Spencer W. Kimball taught:

There are in our lives reservoirs of many kinds. Some reservoirs are to store water. Some are to store food, as we do in our family welfare program and as Joseph did in the land of Egypt during the seven years of plenty. There should also be reservoirs of knowledge to meet the future needs; reservoirs of courage to overcome the floods of fear that put uncertainty in lives; reservoirs of physical strength to help us meet the frequent burdens of work and illness; reservoirs of goodness; reservoirs of stamina; reservoirs of faith. Yes, especially reservoirs of faith so that when the world presses in upon us, we stand firm and strong; when the temptations of a decaying world about us draw on our energies, sap our spiritual vitality, and seek to pull us down, we need a storage of faith that can carry youth and later adults over the dull, the difficult, the terrifying moments, disappointments, disillusionments, and years of adversity, want, confusion, and frustration. (*Faith Precedes the Miracle,* pp. 110–11.)

Just as reservoirs are filled gradually, our own reserves of strength and endurance are steadily enlarged through consistent effort and continual obedience. Perhaps this is one of the most important applications of the Savior's parable of the ten virgins (see Matthew 25:1–13). Although directly related to the preparedness required for the Savior's second coming, the parable also teaches the importance of the ongoing spiritual preparedness necessary to surmount life's many challenges. Elder Kimball elaborated on the message of this important parable.

All of the virgins, wise and foolish, had accepted the invitation to the wedding supper; they had knowledge of the program and had been warned of the important day to come. They were not . . . necessarily corrupt and reprobate, but they were knowing people who were foolishly unprepared for the vital happenings that were to affect their eternal lives.

They had the saving, exalting gospel, but it had not been made the center of their lives. They knew the way but gave only a small measure of loyalty and devotion.
. . .

The foolish [virgins] asked the others to share their oil, but spiritual preparedness cannot be shared in an instant. The wise [virgins] had to go, else the bridegroom would have gone unwelcomed. They needed all their oil for themselves; they could not save the foolish. The responsibility was each for himself.

This was not selfishness or unkindness. The kind of oil that is needed to illuminate the way and light up the darkness is not shareable. How can one share obedience to the principle of tithing; a mind at peace from righteous living; an accumulation of knowledge? How can one share faith or testimony? How can one share attitudes or chastity, or the experience of a mission? How can one share temple privileges? Each must obtain that kind of oil for himself. . . .

In the parable, oil can be purchased at the market. In our lives the oil of preparedness is accumulated drop by drop in righteous living. Attendance at sacrament meetings adds oil to our lamps, drop by drop over the years. Fasting, family prayer, home teaching, control of bodily appetites, preaching the gospel, studying the scriptures—each act of dedication and obedience is a drop added to our store. Deeds of kindness, payment of offerings and tithes, chaste thoughts and actions, marriage in the covenant for eternity—these, too, contribute importantly to the oil with which we can at midnight refuel our exhausted lamps. (*Faith Precedes the Miracle,* pp. 254–56.)

The old adage, "An ounce of prevention is worth a pound of cure," aptly applies to our approach to adversity. Walking uprightly before the Lord and honoring our covenants with him in the bright times of comfort and calm fortify us against the day when we must do battle with dark moments of discouragement and despair. As Phillips Brooks, a nineteenth-century American religious leader and author of the hymn "O Little Town of Bethlehem," insightfully stated: "Someday, in years to come, you'll be wrestling with the great temptation, or trembling under the great sorrow, of your life. But the real struggle is here, now, in these quiet weeks. Now it is being decided whether in the day of your supreme sorrow or temptation, you shall miserably fail or gloriously conquer. Character cannot be made except by a steady, long-continued process."

"Press Forward, Feasting upon the Word of Christ"

Our spiritual reservoirs of endurance-enabling strength are also expanded through consistent study of the scriptures. "Search the scriptures," was the command Jesus gave to the people—both in ancient and modern times (see John 5:39; 3 Nephi 10:14; D&C 1:37). Rich rewards and "hidden treasures" await those who heed the command and diligently search the scriptures. "The holy scriptures," wrote the Apostle Paul to Timothy, "are able to make thee wise unto salvation through faith which is in Christ Jesus. All scripture is given by inspiration of God, and is profitable for doctrine, for reproof, for correction, for instruction in righteousness: that the man of God may be perfect, throughly furnished unto all good works." (2 Timothy 3:15–17.) Although implicit in his statement, perhaps Paul could have appropriately added, "profitable for comfort and guidance in times of trial and tribulation."

As we study the scriptures we vicariously experience the troubles and ultimate triumphs of other men and women who, in time of need, sought strength and courage from the Lord. We read soul-soothing words of comfort spoken by the Lord to those in distress, and they enter sweetly into our own hearts and minds as if spoken directly to us. We find examples to emulate and helpful measures to take in easing our own burdens. Elder Spencer W. Kimball taught:

> We learn the lessons of life more readily and surely if we see the results of wickedness and righteousness in the

lives of others. To know the patriarchs and prophets of ages past and their faithfulness under stress and temptation and persecution strengthens [resolve]. To come to know Job well and intimately is to learn to keep faith through the greatest of adversities. . . . To see the forbearance and fortitude of Paul when he was giving his life to his ministry is to give courage to those who feel they have been injured and tried. . . .

All through the scriptures every weakness and strength of man has been portrayed, and rewards and punishments have been recorded. One would surely be blind who could not learn to live life properly by such reading. The Lord said, "Search the scriptures; for in them ye think ye have eternal life: and they are they which testify of me." (John 5:39.) And it was this same Lord and master in whose life we find every quality of goodness: godliness, strength, controls, perfection. And how can students study this great story without capturing some of it in their lives? (*Teachings of Spencer W. Kimball*, pp. 131–33.)

In addition to learning lessons of life from the examples of people in the scriptures, we will find there is indeed a very real spiritual power that flows into our lives through scripture study, a power that will help shield us against the soul-searing heat of the furnace of affliction. Mormon taught that the "word of God, which is quick and powerful . . . shall divide asunder all the cunning and the snares and the wiles of the devil, and lead the man of Christ in a strait and narrow course across that everlasting gulf of misery" (Helaman 3:29). In the anguish of adversity, when we may feel all alone in our suffering, one of our greatest needs is to feel nearness to God. The Prophet Joseph Smith taught that through studying and abiding by the precepts of the Book of Mormon "a man would get nearer to God . . . than by any other book" (Book of Mormon Introduction, 1981 edition). Elder Kimball testified from personal experience that feelings of forsakenness can be diminished or dispelled through studying the scriptures: "I find that when I get casual in my relationships with divinity and when it seems that no divine ear is listening and no divine voice is speaking, that I am far, far away. If I immerse myself in the scriptures the distance narrows and the spirituality returns." (*Teachings of Spencer W. Kimball,* p. 135.)

This nearness to God resulting from study of the scriptures yields indispensible strength in times of suffering. Through fasting and prayer, and no doubt through this literal transforming power of the word of God, the Nephite Saints "did wax stronger and stronger in their humility, and firmer and firmer in the faith of Christ, unto the filling their souls with joy and consolation" (Helaman 3:35). Jacob taught that the "pleasing word of God"—the scriptures and the words of the prophets—possesses a power "which healeth the wounded soul" (see Jacob 2:8).

We, too, can be blessed beneficiaries of this consoling and healing power of the word. If we will diligently and consistently "press forward, feasting upon the word of Christ" (2 Nephi 31:20), we will hear the voice of the Lord (see D&C 18:34–36) and, as President Kimball promised, "we shall indeed find answers to our problems and peace in our hearts. We shall experience the Holy Ghost broadening our understanding, find new insights, . . . and the doctrines of the Lord shall come to have more meaning to us than we ever thought possible." (*Teachings of Spencer W. Kimball,* p. 135.) President Ezra Taft Benson has also added his prophetic promise of the power of the scriptures in helping us to endure well:

> Many a man in his hour of trial has turned to the Book of Mormon and been enlightened, enlivened, and comforted. The psalms in the Old Testament have a special food for the soul of one in distress. In our day we are

blessed with the Doctrine and Covenants, modern revelation. The words of the prophets, particularly the living President of the Church, are crucial reading and can give direction and comfort in an hour when one is down. (*Teachings of Ezra Taft Benson,* p. 40.)

"Bear with Patience Thine Afflictions, and I Will Give unto You Success"

"Be patient in afflictions, for thou shalt have many," the Lord told Joseph Smith, "but endure them, for, lo, I am with thee, even unto the end of thy days" (D&C 24:8). In Liberty Jail, when persecution and privation were at a pinnacle, the Prophet Joseph Smith was painfully reminded, both by his own experience and through the revelations of the Lord, of the necessity of patience in order to endure well. The Lord graphically described the tribulations that Joseph had suffered and would still suffer but reminded him that such affliction was "but for a small moment" (D&C 122:4). The Lord's admonishment to "be patient in tribulation" is an oft-repeated theme in the scriptures (see D&C 31:9; 54:10; 66:9). Under normal circumstances we understand and willingly acknowledge that patience is imperative in the process of perfection, but in times of trouble and turmoil this *head knowledge* may not translate into *heart acceptance.* During seasons of stress and suffering the admonition to "bear with patience thine afflictions" (Alma 26:27) is easier said (and read) than done. Neither is there much consolation in the Lord's assurance that our afflictions are "but for a small moment," when the pain persists much longer than we anticipated or when we remember that, according to the Lord's time, a thousand years is but a day unto him (see Abraham 3:4). Under this eternal reckoning of time it is no wonder that "small moments" can truly try our patience!

Amidst adversity it is natural to be impatient, even when we are sincerely striving to "wait upon the Lord" (Isaiah 40:31). This natural inclination can be characterized by a short saying I first saw on the kitchen wall of my mother's home. It said simply: "God grant me patience—RIGHT NOW!" Someone once cleverly quipped, "Patience is the art of hiding our impatience." Impatience is a trait of the natural man, and just as "the natural man is an enemy to God" (Mosiah 3:19), impatience can become an enemy to spiritual development and faithful endurance. "Patience is tied very closely to faith in our Heavenly Father," stated Elder Neal A. Maxwell. "Actually, when we are unduly impatient we are suggesting that we know what is best—better than does God. Or, at least, we are asserting that our timetable is better than His. Either way we are questioning the reality of God's omniscience as if, as some seem to believe, God were on some sort of postdoctoral fellowship and were not quite in charge of everything."

This attitude of restlessness and disquietude is antithetical to faith and brings with it its own spiritual side effects that make enduring much more difficult. Elder Maxwell compared our natural impatience with "too much anxious opening of the oven door," which causes the cake to fall instead of rise, and with "pulling up the daisies to see how the roots are doing." He explained further:

> When we are impatient, we are neither reverential nor reflective because we are too self-centered. Whereas faith and patience are companions, so are selfishness and impatience. . . .
>
> Clearly, without patience we will learn less in life. We will see less; we will feel less; we will hear less. Ironically, "rush" and "more" usually mean "less." The pressure of "now," time and time again, goes against the grain of the gospel with its eternalism.

There is also in patience a greater opportunity for that discernment which sorts out the things that matter most from the things that matter least. ("Patience," pp. 215–18.)

Recognizing the pitfalls of impatience leaves us with the important question of how we can develop the cardinal attribute of patience—"Lord, how is it done?" There are neither easy answers to this question nor step-by-step programs for developing patience, but we can discover simple yet significant things that we can do to acquire patience and more fully exercise it in our days of distress and discouragement.

One of the best ways we can cultivate patience is to live and focus on one day or even one moment at a time, while leaning upon the grace of God to help us through and being thankful for the good days and making the best of the bad. When we worry about the future, afraid of how long our sojourn in suffering will last, we become anxious, then overwhelmed, then discouraged—even despairing. Enduring adversity is like any journey in that the pathway from pain to peace must be taken one step at a time. Just as dwelling on past problems and mistakes retards spiritual growth, so can our present strength be sapped and our power to endure diminished when we constantly dwell too anxiously on the future—when we stew over what may be in store for us and languish in our desires to have the burden lifted. Dwelling needlessly or negatively on either the past or the future prevents us from utilizing our experiences and circumstances to bless the present. "Patience helps us to use, rather than to protest, [the] seeming flat periods of life," Elder Maxwell observed, "becoming filled with quiet wonder over the past and with anticipation for that which may lie ahead, instead of demeaning the particular flatness through which we may be passing at the time" ("Patience," p. 217). Patience requires waiting—not passive waiting, foolish fretting, or idle twiddling of our thumbs, but waiting on the Lord. "Wait on the Lord," the Psalmist wrote, "be of good courage, and he shall strengthen thine heart: wait, I say, on the Lord" (Psalm 27:14). Waiting on the Lord implies active submissiveness to his ultimate designs for our lives.

Submissiveness, which King Benjamin characterized as being "willing to submit to all things which the Lord seeth fit to inflict upon [us], even as a child doth submit to his father" (Mosiah 3:19), also produces and strengthens adversity-enduring patience. Patiently submitting to the Lord's will means humbly accepting not only the "what" but also the "when" and the "how long." Trials and tribulations bring us to our knees until we stop resisting and surrender our lives over to the Lord. Only through such liberating surrender can we find the promised peace amidst affliction. Elder Maxwell taught that such submissive patience "cradles us when we are in the midst of suffering" and helps us realize that "we are actually being helped even as we cry for help" ("Patience," pp. 217–18).

Patience ultimately helps us progress in our lives. "Bear with patience thine afflictions," the Lord told Ammon and his brethren, "and I will give unto you success" (Alma 26:27). We, too, can achieve success if we let patience carry us through our trials and move us forward. In the words of Elder Maxwell: "Patient endurance permits us to cling to our faith in the Lord and our faith in His timing when we are being tossed about by the surf of circumstance. Even when a seeming undertow grasps us, somehow, in the tumbling, we are being carried forward, though battered and bruised." (" 'Endure It Well,' " p. 34.)

"Bear One Another's Burdens, That They May Be Light"

When we are struggling under the burdens of our own suffering and sorrow, we may feel we have little strength or desire to reach out in service to others. This natural inclination to withdraw ourselves and recoil from service while we introspectively "regroup" or "lick our own wounds" poses a very real threat to personal spirituality — spirituality so desperately needed in order to remain true during the tempests of tribulation. "If we are not careful, we can be injured by the frostbite of frustration," stated President Spencer W. Kimball, quoting another General Authority. "We can be frozen in place by the chill of unmet expectations. To avoid this we must — just as we would with arctic coldness — keep moving, keep serving, and keep reaching out, so that our own immobility does not become our chief danger." (In "Small Acts of Service," p. 4.)

One of the most helpful and healing actions we can take in times of adversity is to extend ourselves beyond our own problems by lifting and strengthening others. "Those to whom true joy comes," someone once observed, "have windows in their lives, not mirrors." Without losing any of the original meaning, this maxim certainly could be paraphrased and expanded to say: "Suffering souls seeking peace and comfort find it through selfless service, not through self-pity."

The covenantal obligation resting upon all of us to "bear one another's burdens, that they may be light" (Mosiah 18:8), and to "succor the weak, lift up the hands which hang down, and strengthen the feeble knees" (D&C 81:5) is neither rescinded nor suspended during times of distress and discouragement. If anything, that obligation is

intensified during times of adversity—not so much because of what we can do for others, but because of what
that service can do for us. Elder Dean L. Larsen affirmed
that giving of ourselves to lift others is one of the most significant things that we can do to find comfort in times of
tribulation and to experience ''the peaceable things of the
kingdom'' (D&C 39:6).

> Raise your own spirits by finding something to do that will
> lift others. Nothing seems to have a greater power for
> turning us away from our own self-pity and despondency
> than to focus upon something good we can do for someone
> else who has a need.
>   Erich Fromm has said:
>
>> The most important sphere of giving . . . is not that
>> of material things, but lies in the specifically human
>> realm. What does one person give to another? He gives
>> of himself, of the most precious he has, he gives of his
>> life. This does not necessarily mean that he sacrifices
>> his life for the other—but that he gives him of that
>> which is alive in him; he gives him of his joy, of his in-
>> terest, of his understanding, of his knowledge, of his
>> humor, of his sadness—of all expressions and mani-
>> festations of that which is alive in him. . . . He does
>> not give in order to receive; giving is in itself exquisite
>> joy. But in giving he cannot help bringing something to
>> life in the other person, and this which is brought to
>> life reflects back to him; in truly giving, he cannot help
>> receiving that which is given back to him. [*The Art of
>> Loving* (New York: Bantam Books, Inc., 1970), p.
>> 20–21.]
>
>   . . . I think there is nothing we can do to develop
> godlike qualities that is more important than giving of our-
> selves [in service to others]. . . . And I believe it has some
> of the highest prospects for helping us overcome any un-

happiness we may be experiencing ourselves. ("The Peaceable Things of the Kingdom," pp. 74–75.)

The Savior taught that one's life is found through losing it in service to others (see Matthew 10:39). This finding through losing concept can also be applied directly to enduring adversity and triumphing over tragedies. Through "bearing one another's burdens" our pains and problems "lose" much of their sting, and our troubles and trials "lose" much of their terror. I have personally experienced this process many times in my life but perhaps never more profoundly than during my service as a bishop. While struggling with my own difficulties, I often comforted, counseled, and sought to strengthen ward members who were grappling with their problems. These problems included marital and family troubles, terminal illnesses and other serious health concerns, financial collapses, and the burdensome by-products of sin. Upon coming home from hospitals, homes, or the bishop's office, I was always able to look upon my own problems in a different light. The discomforts of my own trials seemed dull in comparison to the heartaches of those whom I served. This new view of adversity substantially increased my gratitude to the Lord. I found myself appreciating blessings I enjoy rather than bemoaning burdens I must bear. In addition to this broadened perspective, I often found answers to my prayers, guidance for my own life, and comfort for myself through things that were said and done in behalf of others. President Spencer W. Kimball declared:

I have learned that it is by serving that we learn how to serve. When we are engaged in the service of our fellowmen, not only do our deeds assist them, but we put our own problems in a fresher perspective. When we concern ourselves more with others, there is less time to be concerned with ourselves. In the midst of the miracle of serving, there is the promise of Jesus, that by losing ourselves, we find ourselves (see Matthew 10:39).

Not only do we "find" ourselves in terms of acknowledging guidance in our lives, but the more we serve our fellowmen in appropriate ways, the more substance there is to our souls. We become more significant individuals as we serve others. We become more substantive as we serve others—indeed, it is easier to "find" ourselves because there is so much more of us to find! . . .

God does notice us, and he watches over us. But it is usually through another person that he meets our needs. . . . So often, our acts of service consist of simple encouragement or of giving mundane help with mundane tasks, but what glorious consequences can flow from mundane acts and from small but deliberate deeds! ("Small Acts of Service," pp. 2, 5.)

Sometimes our suffering seems senseless. We can more clearly discern the designs of God in our afflictions when we remember that the painful lessons of adversity need not be wasted. "The dues of discipleship are high indeed," observed Elder Neal A. Maxwell, "and how much we can *take* so often determines how much we can then *give*" ("Patience," p. 218). Through engendering in us an empathy and an increased desire to help others bear their burdens, our personal afflictions uniquely qualify us to succor fellow sufferers. By virtue of the knowledge gained from painful "homework" in the "school of suffering," we can now tutor others with superb sensitivity, whereas once we may not have even noticed, cared, or known what could be done.

At times it may be impossible, because of the nature of our trials, to render all the service and deeds of compassion that we desire to render. During these times we must remember that our endurance-enhancing service may take on a new form—that of allowing others to serve and learn from us. We likewise must learn all we can from our trying circumstances and recognize that we are being schooled for subsequent service.

Comfort and strength to endure come as we help others endure. Of this the Apostle Paul testified: "Blessed be God, even the Father of our Lord Jesus Christ, the Father of mercies, and the God of all comfort; who comforteth us in all our tribulation, that we may be able to comfort them which are in any trouble, by the comfort wherewith we ourselves are comforted of God" (2 Corinthians 1:3-4).

"Ye May Know That He Is, by the Power of the Holy Ghost"

Obtaining and maintaining an unshakable testimony of the gospel of Jesus Christ are essential elements for endurance of adversity. In our "hope to be able to endure all things" we are strengthened and instructed by the exemplary suffering of those who "have endured many things." The scriptures and the history of the latter-day Church are replete with accounts of those who endured all manner of tribulation and willingly laid their all upon the altar of God. Each of these individuals was able to do so because of the witness of the Spirit that so powerfully burned within his or her soul and testified of truthfulness and Truth—the truthfulness of the gospel and the divinity of the Savior, the Truth of the world (see John 14:6).

In the Bible and the Book of Mormon, examples abound of righteous Saints who, because of their testimonies of the gospel, were able to endure pains, prisons, perplexities, hardships, heartaches, and heavy burdens.

Perhaps the Apostle Paul exemplifies all such faithful Saints. After his conversion Paul experienced all manner of problems and persecutions—whippings, illness, loss of friends, false accusations, and so on. Despite all this he remained true and faithful to the testimony he had received: "But what things were gain to me, those I counted loss for Christ. Yea doubtless, and I count all things but loss for the excellency of the knowledge of Christ Jesus my Lord: for whom I have suffered the loss of all things, and do count them but dung, that I may win Christ." (Philippians 3:7-8.)

In this dispensation the early Saints sacrificed comfortable homes and prospering businesses in order to gather with the Saints in Zion. Persecution became the cost of their conversion and the price of their discipleship. The hardships encountered on the pioneer trail were willingly accepted and faithfully endured by the Saints because a testimony of the restored gospel and of a living prophet burned within their hearts. Not unlike our pioneer forefathers there are some among us today who, when faced with life's many challenges, have strength to endure because they have diligently obtained and consistently maintained a testimony of the restored gospel. One such example is Pablo Choc, who was president of the Patzicia Branch during the 1976 Guatemalan earthquake. An account of his experience during that earthquake appeared in the *Church News*:

> At the same time the fearsome earthquake was knocking the supporting beam on top of Elder Randall Ellsworth while the young missionary was sleeping in the Patzicia Branch cultural hall, it was tumbling the walls of Pres. Choc's home, killing his wife, a young son and daughter. After he had seen to the needs of his family, and taken care of the bodies of his wife and two children, Pres. Choc immediately went to the branch chapel to check on the

damage there. At the building he assisted in freeing Elder Ellsworth and helped transport the missionary to Guatemala City for medical aid, knowing all the while that his beloved wife and children lay dead back in Patzicia.

[Pres. Choc later stated,] "I am of course saddened by the death of my wife and children, . . . and I will miss her in helping to raise our six remaining children. We were married very young, and in all those years of marriage we never had a real problem. Then in the three weeks after her death I did a lot of praying to the Lord, more than I had ever done before, and I found a lot of strength in my prayers and felt myself getting closer to the Lord. . . . Because of this I don't think my faith ever weakened or wavered for a moment."

During this time the Chocs' eldest son, Daniel, had been called on a mission and had been teaching the American missionaries the Mayan dialect so proselyting could be stepped up in the mission district. As a result of the earthquake, the missionaries had been assigned to assist in the cleanup work with the members of the Church in their area. Elder Choc was cleaning up the inside of a home as an aftershock occurred. His companion and two other missionaries scrambled to safety, but Elder Choc was trapped by a falling wall and killed. As Pres. Choc talked about the deaths in his family, tears began to well in his eyes and slowly slide down his dirt-stained face.

"I was sad, very sad when Daniel was killed, but in a way I am very happy. There are so many of my Mayan people on the other side that Daniel, his mother and the other two children are spending their time teaching them the Gospel message in their native language, and they are spending their time serving the Lord. . . . This is really the Lord's work." (Jay Livingood, "Quake's Heavy Hand Didn't Crush Testimony," p. 5.)

A testimony is not only essential for initial conversion and acceptance of the gospel, but it is also a continual source of strength throughout life. There will be times when our testimonies may be the only thing upon which we can surely rest. Perhaps Jesus' parable of the foolish man who built his house on sand and the wise man who built his on rock (see Matthew 7:24–27) can be appropriately applied to the importance of personal testimony. Without our own witness of the truthfulness of the gospel we, like the foolish man, will see our spiritual foundation crumble like a sand castle against the waves.

President Heber C. Kimball prophesied of coming difficulties that would threaten the Church collectively and identified the needed fortification against such an assault. No doubt his prophecy also includes insight into how we can meet our individual difficulties. "To meet the difficulties that are coming, it will be necessary for you to have a knowledge of the truth of this work for yourselves. The difficulties will be of such a character that the man or woman who does not possess this personal knowledge or witness will fall. . . . The time will come when no man nor woman will be able to endure on borrowed light. Each will have to be guided by the light within himself. If you do not have it, how can you stand?" (As quoted in Orson F. Whitney, *Life of Heber C. Kimball,* p. 450.)

"Ye may know that he is, by the power of the Holy Ghost" (Moroni 10:7). Merely ascertaining *if* we have ever received such a witness may not be enough; we also need to evaluate *when* we last enjoyed a spiritual witness and how reliable that testimony is today. Gaining a testimony only at conversion—or on our mission, or the first time we read the Book of Mormon—may not produce the endurance needed to overcome the obstacles of adversity. "Testimony isn't something you have today, and you are going to have always," explained President Harold B. Lee. "A testimony is fragile. It is as hard to hold as a moonbeam. It is something you have to recapture every day of your life." (*Church News,* 15 July 1972, p. 4.) As we first *obtain* a testimony and then consistently *maintain* that testimony, our endurance capacity is increased and our spiritual foundation is fortified.

A general testimony should include specific testimonies of the divine mission of the Prophet Joseph Smith, of the veracity of the Book of Mormon, and of the truthfulness of the Church. These are vital elements of the "rock foundation" upon which our lives must be built in order to endure well the adversities and oppositions in mortality. Each of these elements testifies of and points us to the central element of testimony, characterized by Helaman as "a sure foundation":

> Remember, remember that it is upon the rock of our Redeemer, who is Christ, the Son of God, that ye must build your foundation; that when the devil shall send forth his mighty winds, yea, his shafts in the whirlwind, yea, when all his hail and his mighty storm shall beat upon you, it shall have no power over you to drag you down to the gulf of misery and endless wo, because of the rock upon which ye are built, which is a sure foundation, a foundation whereon if men build they cannot fall (Helaman 5:12).

"In the World Ye Shall Have Tribulation: But Be of Good Cheer"

The Savior's inspired injunction to "be of good cheer" amidst the agony of adversity and the terrors of tribulation seems, at first glance, to be a painful paradox. How can good cheer exist simultaneously with sorrow, suffering, tears, and trials? Good cheer seems, on the surface, to be totally at odds with the normal emotional upheaval that stems from the troublesome and tragic circumstances in which we may find ourselves. Sometimes good cheer is perceived only in terms of a positive mental attitude that supposedly should chase away all heartache. "Just put on a happy face" and your problems and pain will automatically go away, some may think. Such a superficial view of this important scriptural concept may actually hurt rather than heal. This unrealistic "positive attitude," or "counterfeit cheer," may actually make some people feel guilty or faithless when they honestly recognize, confront, and/or express their emotions of sadness and discouragement. It must be remembered that the Lord does not desire us to sweep our sorrows under a rug, as it were, nor does he intend that we ignore our injuries, feign feelings of happiness, or pretend that our problems do not exist. The genuine spirit of good cheer allows for all of the emotions of adversity—sorrow, pain, discouragement, anger, frustration; the good cheer that the Savior admonishes us to have does not imply that we must suppress such sentiments but rather that we must deal with them in a way that promotes emotional healing and spiritual growth. Elder Boyd K. Packer declared: "Did you know that it is normal and healthy to be depressed occasionally? . . . If you happen to hit a good sorry mood once in a while, relax and enjoy it —it is a good sign that you are normal." (*"Let Not Your Heart Be Troubled . . ."* [address], p. 6.) Using the poem entitled "Smile, Darned You, Smile," Elder Packer went on to cleverly illustrate the shallowness and futility of the "just put on a happy face" attitude:

> If you can smile when things go wrong
> And say it doesn't matter,
> If you can laugh off cares and woe
> And troubles make you fatter,
> If you can keep a cheerful face
> When all around are blue,
> Then have your head examined, bud,

> There's something wrong with you.
> For one thing I've arrived at:
> There are no ands and buts,
> A guy that's grinning all the time
> Must be completely nuts.
> (As quoted in *"Let Not Your Heart Be Troubled . . ."* [address], p. 6.)

Simply pasting a smile over sorrow or making the trite suggestion to those who suffer, "Don't worry—be happy," may seem appealing as ways to clothe ourselves in a sort of emotional armor that protects us from being pierced by pain. "But at what cost?" asked Rabbi Kushner. Such an attitude of detachment, he suggests, "immunizes me against great pain but also serves to rob me of great hope and great joy. . . . Putting on the armor keeps us from being hurt, but it also keeps us from growing. And yet we have to grow." (*When All You've Ever Wanted Isn't Enough,* pp. 92–93. See copyright and permission information, p. 69 herein.)

Good cheer incorporates genuine contentment and a positive outlook on life. It is much more, however, than an external expression of cheerfulness alone. It is a profound *inward* strength and confidence, tempered by trust in the Lord and hope for humanity, that permeates one's actions as well as one's attitude. To be of good cheer is to perceive, from an eternal perspective, the purpose of pain and problems and to be "content with the things which the Lord hath allotted" (Alma 29:3). "Good cheer is a state of mind or mood that promotes happiness or joy," taught Elder Marvin J. Ashton.

> With God's help, good cheer permits us to rise above the depressing present or difficult circumstances. It is a process of positive reassurance and reinforcement. It is sunshine when clouds block the light.

Recently, while visiting with a wife who had suddenly lost her husband through a tragic death, I was touched . . . when she said, "My heart is heavy and sad, but my soul is of good cheer." There was a powerful inward cheer dominating the sorrowful situation. The promise "for I the Lord am with you" was triumphing over heartache and despair. People of good cheer soften the sorrows of others as well as those that weigh mightily upon themselves.

None of us will escape tragedy and suffering. Each of us will probably react differently. However, if we can recall the Lord's promise "for I the Lord am with you," we will be able to face our problems with dignity and courage. We will find the strength to be of good cheer instead of becoming resentful, critical, or defeated. We will be able to meet life's unpleasant happenings with clear vision, strength, and power. . . .

. . . When we apply this principle in our lives and share it with our associates, it is possible to supplant discouragement, tragedy, and gloom with hope and cheer. . . .

Good cheer is best [obtained and] shared by those who will discard fear, cheerfully accept what comes and use it wisely, become converted, obey the commandments of God, avoid self-deceit and rationalization.

Being of good cheer makes it possible for us to turn all of our sunsets into sunrises. With good cheer, carrying our cross can be our ladder to happiness. When Jesus comes into our lives, cheer lights the way. (*Be of Good Cheer*, pp. 1–2, 7.)

Another important aspect of being of good cheer that will help us through the difficult and distressing moments of mortality is maintaining a healthy sense of humor. "I do not believe the Lord intends and desires that we should pull a long face and look sanctimonious and hypocritical," said President Joseph Fielding Smith. "I think he expects us to be happy and of a cheerful countenance." (As quoted in Hoyt W. Brewster Jr., "It's OK to Be Spiritual and Still Have Fun," p. 11). The familiar saying, "Laughter is the best medicine," is not just a clever quotation but also a potent prescription that helps heal. Good cheer prevents us from losing the laughter that can lighten burdens and dispel dark clouds of despair that come into our lives. A character in a memorable movie thoughtfully remarked, "Laughter through tears is my favorite emotion." Elder J. Golden Kimball often used his keen humor to deal with difficult and stressful circumstances and regularly tried to get the Saints to "lighten up" and recognize the spiritual benefits of humor and laughter. "The Lord, Himself, must like a joke," he once quipped, "or He wouldn't have made some of you people" (in Brewster, "It's OK," p. 11).

President Spencer W. Kimball, who was intimately acquainted with sorrow and sickness, knew how to use humor to make suffering bearable. As a lad he was stricken with Bell's palsy, which left half his face paralyzed, yet he joked that speaking under such a circumstance was "a one-sided affair" (in Edward L. Kimball and Andrew E. Kimball Jr., *Spencer W. Kimball*, p. 40). After his call to the apostleship he was diagnosed as having throat cancer. Despite surgery and the difficult and arduous rehabilitation, he jested about the experience and characterized it by saying that he had "fallen among cutthroats." When he was forced by many physical maladies to take several different medications, he referred to himself as " 'the piller' of the Church." Late in his life he hid his anxiety about being unable to carry out his responsibilities by joking with his wife, Camilla, about "the old machine wearing out" and their "hillside cemetery plots waiting with a marvelous view of the valley." (In *Spencer W. Kimball*, pp. 311, 425–26.) With his beloved sense of humor he lightened not only his own burdens but ours as well. If a prophet of the Lord can laugh at himself in the midst of his many trying moments, surely we can too.

Even in the suffering that defies human comprehension, humor helps give life meaning and makes endurance possible. "Humor was another of the soul's weapons in the fight for self-preservation," wrote Viktor E. Frankl in regards to his enduring the inhuman conditions he faced as a prisoner in Nazi concentration camps in World War II. "It is well known that humor, more than anything else in the human make-up, can afford aloofness and an ability to rise above any situation, even if only for a few seconds." (*Man's Search for Meaning,* p. 63.) Maintaining a sense of humor is as essential to good cheer as good cheer is to being able to endure well. Author Romain Gary's profound statement seems to summarize it best: "Humor is an affirmation of dignity, a declaration of man's superiority to all that befalls him" (in A. K. Adams, ed., *The Book of Humorous Quotations,* p. 173).

There is another aspect of good cheer—a deeply spiritual aspect—that constitutes the substance from which stems our lasting strength to endure and our abiding courage to overcome. The Savior specifically identified this spiritual source of good cheer, or source that ultimately enables one to endure faithfully. To his Apostles he declared: "These things I have spoken unto you, that *in me ye might have peace.* In the world ye shall have tribulation: but be of good cheer; I have overcome the world." (John 16:33, italics added.) From this divine declaration we see that good cheer—that which we are charged to have and to exercise in the tumultuous times of tribulation—comes from and centers in Christ. The good cheer of which Jesus spoke is a product of the "good tidings of great joy" spoken of by an angel at the time of Jesus' birth (Luke 2:10). "And this is the . . . glad tidings," we read in a modern revelation, "that he came into the world, even

Jesus, to be crucified for the world, and to bear the sins of the world, and to sanctify the world, and to cleanse it from all unrighteousness" (D&C 76:40–41). Elder Neal A. Maxwell characterized this Christ-centered good cheer as follows:

> Being of good cheer . . . is not naivete concerning conditions in the world—nor is it superficiality in reacting to the rigors of life. It is a deliberate attitudinal and intellectual posture, a deep trust in God's unfolding purposes—not only for all of mankind, but for each of us as individuals. Indeed, this attribute which Jesus spoke of might well be called "gospel gladness." It involves being constantly aware, and appreciative, of the ultimate justifications for our being of good cheer. Gospel gladness places the proximate frustrations and tribulations in needed perspective. If, however, our good cheer depends too much on the outcome of an election, or an athletic contest, or having a good date, or on interest rates coming down, or the outcome of a sales contest, then our moods are too much at the mercy of men and circumstance. There are, to be sure, proximate things over which we can and should rightfully rejoice, but it is the ultimate things over which we can be of lasting good cheer. Note what Jesus said to the Twelve in this powerful scripture: "These things I have spoken unto you, that in me ye might have peace. In the world ye shall have tribulation: but be of good cheer; I have overcome the world." (John 16:33.) How was it possible for the Twelve to be of good cheer? The unimaginable agony of Gethsemane was about to descend upon Jesus; Judas' betrayal was imminent. Then would come Jesus' arrest and arraignment; the scattering of the Twelve like sheep; the awful scourging of the Savior; the unjust trial; the mob's shrill cry for Barabbas instead of Jesus; and then the awful crucifixion on Calvary. What was there to be cheerful about? Just what Jesus said: He had overcome the world! The atonement was about to be a

reality. The resurrection of all mankind was assured. Death was to be done away with—Satan had failed to stop the atonement. These are the fundamental facts. These are the resplendent realities over which we are to be of good cheer, even in the midst of the disappointments of the day. [We all need] to focus on these basic things which are firmly and irrevocably in place. Then [we] can better cope with the frustrations and the tactical tribulations of the moment. (*But a Few Days*, p. 4.)

"Let Thy Mercy, O Lord, Be upon Us, According as We Hope in Thee"

"Out of the mouth of babes and sucklings," declared the Psalmist, "hast thou ordained strength" (Psalm 8:2). Sometimes we are able to glean perfect instruction and renewed resolve from the simple, faith-filled utterances of children. Such was the case as our youngest daughter, Emma Jane, taught us a lesson about hope. Emma Jane developed a deep friendship with our next-door neighbors' daughter, Kori, who was paralyzed and confined to a wheelchair. Kori is a beautiful young woman whose spine had been severely injured in a tragic car accident when she was a teenager. Almost every day Emma Jane would go to Kori's house to talk with her, brush her hair, polish her nails, and just be around her. Each night this little four-year-old would say in her prayers, "Heavenly Father, please bless Kori that she will be able to walk again." We had explained to little Janie the physiological effects of Kori's accident and that she would indeed walk again, but not in this life. Despite our best explanations, Janie continued to pray each night that her friend would be able to walk and run. After one of Janie's prayers, my wife again reminded her that in mortality Kori would probably not ever walk again. "I know that," Emma Jane responded firmly. Then, somewhat matter-of-factly, she added, "But I can still hope."

At the time of this writing, two years later, Emma Jane continues to pray for Kori's legs, even though Kori has moved away and is still in a wheelchair. This example of a child's unwavering faith and pure hope testified to me that we must hold tightly to hope despite earthly circumstances and human explanations. It is this kind of hope that buoys the human spirit, propels man forward, and strengthens his capacity to endure even the most unbearable circumstances.

The scriptural meaning of hope implies much more than mere wishing or escapism. It is an eternal expectation, an abiding confidence in the fulfillment of God's promises and covenants. It is an inner peace resulting from a personal relationship with Deity (see G. W. Bromiley, ed., *The International Standard Bible Encyclopedia* 2:751–55). Paul spoke of this hope as "an anchor of the soul" which brings "strong consolation" and "refuge" amidst adversity and affliction (see Hebrews 6:18–19). In a related vein Paul also taught that without a hope in all of the blessings of Christ's atonement, "we are of all men most miserable" (1 Corinthians 15:19).

The Book of Mormon also teaches and testifies of hope as a source of strength and solace. Nephi spoke of the necessity of having "a perfect brightness of hope" (2 Nephi 31:20). Ether taught his people to "hope for a better world" and promised that this spiritual, faith-centered hope "maketh an anchor to the souls of men, which [will] make them sure and steadfast" (Ether 12:4). This "hope for a better world" should not be viewed as passively putting up with the pains and problems of this life and biding one's time until the glorious resurrection; hope involves overcoming our fears by also hoping for a better world *in this life*—by hoping that good things will happen to us. We should stop worrying about all the things that may go wrong and trust that our lives will be rich and rewarding. Most of the things we worry about never come to pass. "How much pain never-occurred evils cost us!" Thomas Jefferson once remarked. Hope implies *expecting* that the future will be better and brighter.

"Blessed is the man," declared the prophet Jeremiah, "that trusteth in the Lord, and whose hope the Lord is. For he shall be as a tree planted by the waters, and that spreadeth out her roots by the river, and shall not see [fear] when heat [adversity] cometh, but her leaf shall be green; and shall not be careful in the year of drought, neither shall cease from yielding fruit." (Jeremiah 17:7–8.) And in the Book of Psalms we read, "Let thy mercy, O Lord, be upon us, according as we hope in thee" (Psalm 33:22). In the scriptural sense it is the Savior that gives life and meaning to the concept of hope. He is in very deed "the hope of Israel, the saviour thereof in time of trouble" (Jeremiah 14:8). When we center our hope in Christ, it is this assurance of what he *is*, what he *has done,* and how he *continues* to love and lift us that swallows up wishful thinking and replaces it with active expectation—that is, with "a lively hope," as Peter described it: "Blessed be the God and Father of our Lord Jesus Christ, which according to his abundant mercy hath begotten us gain unto a lively hope by the resurrection of Jesus Christ from the dead. . . . Wherein ye greatly rejoice, though now for a season, if need be, ye are in heaviness through manifold temptations [i.e., trials, afflictions]." (1 Peter 1:3, 6.)

In our own day, Church leaders continue to emphasize the need for hope. Elder John H. Groberg testified of the soul-strengthening power of hope—even a "perfect brightness of hope" that is founded firmly upon and flows freely from the atonement of Jesus Christ.

A person without hope is like a person without a heart; there is nothing to keep him going. As the heart gives life to the body, so it seems that hope is an enlivening influence to the spirit. . . . The basis of all righteous hope is the person of our Lord and Savior Jesus Christ. In Him all hope has its existence. Without Him there is no hope. But because He was and is and ever will be, there was, is, and ever will be hope—hope in all areas. He is hope. . . .

. . . In Christ who lives and loves and works miracles now, there is always hope. Listen again and again and again. There is always hope—now, today. There is always hope. He lives. He loves. He saves. In Him there is always hope. . . .

To all those who ask the plaintive question, "Is there any hope for me?" the answer is a resounding, "Yes! There is always hope." Reverberating through all eternity, all creation exults: "In Christ there is always hope."

Seek after Him in all ways and at all times until you can sense His smiling countenance saying to you, "Come unto me and I will give you rest. I am the hope of the world. In me there is always hope." ("There Is Always Hope," pp. 48, 65, 67.)

"Come Unto Me, . . . and I Will Give You Rest"

There are many things that we can do to increase our spiritual strength so that we can endure hardships, but in the ultimate sense it is what *Christ* does for us, through his love, compassion, and grace, that ensures our triumph over all tribulation. When all attempts to find peace in our hearts and strength in our spirits fall short, we can literally cast our "care upon him; for he careth for [us]" (1 Peter 5:7). Elder Neal A. Maxwell, as quoted in a previous chapter, admonished those who feel all alone in their suffering and sorrows, "Please forgive those of us who clumsily try to comfort you. We know from whence your true comfort comes. God's 'bosom' is there to be leaned upon." (" 'Yet Thou Art There,' " p. 32.) Therefore, ultimately there is only one enduring source of comfort—He who suffered for us. Placing our burdens upon Christ's shoulders and pleading for his caring concern and healing help is no imposition; rather, it is the desired response to his invitation: "come unto me, all ye that labour and are heavy laden, and I will give you rest. Take my yoke upon you, and learn of me; for I am meek and lowly in heart; and ye shall find rest unto your souls. For my yoke is easy, and my burden is light." (Matthew 11:28-30.)

The Prophet Joseph Smith, while languishing in Liberty Jail, learned firsthand that the Savior can indeed extend peace and strength to all who "labour and are heavy laden," because, as regards all of life's tribulations, "the Son of Man hath descended below them all" (D&C 122:8). Jesus can care for and lift us because he has "descended below them all"—experienced, comprehended, and conquered all manner of suffering. He was and is literally "touched with the feeling of our infirmities" (Hebrews 4:15), and because "he himself hath suffered being [tried], he is able to succour them that are [tried]" (Hebrews 2:18). We gain increased strength to endure when we understand that, despite our periodic feelings that no one can comprehend the depths of our sufferings, Jesus understands and can lift those burdens because, in some unfathomable way, he bore them long before we did.

> And he shall go forth, suffering pains and afflictions and temptations of every kind; and this that the word might be fulfilled which saith he will take upon him the pains and sicknesses of his people.
>
> And he will take upon him death, that he may loose the bands of death which bind his people; and he will

take upon him their infirmities, that his bowels may be filled with mercy, according to the flesh, that he may know according to the flesh how to succor his people according to their infirmities. (Alma 7:11-12.)

The Savior's promise to give us rest is real. He will help us endure if we will come unto him and cast our cares upon him. "He will swallow up death in victory; and the Lord God will wipe away tears from off all faces" (Isaiah 25:8). Because Christ has "trodden the wine-press alone" (D&C 76:107), we do not have to tread the trail of tears and tribulation alone. His promises are sure, his promised peace perfect. He will neither fail us nor forsake us. "For can a woman forget her sucking child, that she should not have compassion on the son of her womb? Yea, they may forget, yet will I not forget thee. . . . Behold, I have graven thee upon the palms of my hands." (1 Nephi 21:15-16.) Elder Jeffrey R. Holland has testified of Christ's continuing compassion and of the strength we can receive from him amidst our suffering:

Life has its share of some fear and some failure. Sometimes things fall short, don't quite measure up. Sometimes in both personal and public life, we are seemingly left without strength to go on. Sometimes people fail us, or economies and circumstance fail us, and life with its hardship and heartache can leave us feeling very alone.

But when such difficult moments come to us, I testify that there is one thing which will never, ever fail us. One thing alone will stand the test of all time, of all tribulation, all trouble, and all transgression. One thing only never faileth—and that is the pure love of Christ. . . .

. . . "If ye have not charity, ye are nothing" (Moroni 7:46). Only the pure love of Christ will see us through. It is Christ's love which suffereth long, and is kind. It is Christ's love which is not puffed up nor easily provoked. Only his pure love enables him—and us—to bear all things, believe all things, hope all things, and endure all things. (See Moroni 7:45.)

> Oh, love effulgent, love divine!
> What debt of gratitude is mine,
> That in his off'ring I have part
> And hold a place within his heart.
> (*Hymns*, 1985, no. 187.)

I testify that having loved us who are in the world, Christ loves us to the end. His pure love never fails us. Not now. Not ever. Not ever. (" 'He Loved Them unto the End,' " p. 26.)

CHAPTER FIVE

"The Glory Which Shall Follow"

Job's exemplary endurance of almost unspeakable suffering, both physical and emotional, is a source of strength and inspiration to us in times of trouble. When we read of his pains and problems, our own are placed in proper perspective as we recognize that we, like the Prophet Joseph Smith, are "not yet as Job" (see D&C 121:10). Our willingness to submit to the will of God, to trust in him at all costs, and our capacity to patiently endure our lot in life are also bolstered by reading of Job's unwearying faithfulness. These are some of the beneficial effects of Job's account, but perhaps the most overlooked yet most transcendent contribution of the story of Job is its happy ending. As we read of the results of Job's patient endurance we see, as it were, the windows of heaven opened and the promised blessings being showered upon Job. All of Job's losses—his health, wealth, family, and friends—were restored unto him.

> And the Lord turned the captivity [affliction or suffering] of Job, when he prayed for his friends: also the Lord gave Job twice as much as he had before.
>
> Then came there unto him all his brethren, and all his sisters, and all they that had been of his acquaintance before, and did eat bread with him in his house: and they bemoaned him, and comforted him over all the evil that the Lord had brought upon him: every man also gave him a piece of money, and every one an earring of gold.
>
> So the Lord blessed the latter end of Job more than his beginning: for he had fourteen thousand sheep, and six thousand camels, and a thousand yoke of oxen, and a thousand she asses.
>
> He had also seven sons and three daughters. . . .
>
> And in all the land were no women found so fair as the daughters of Job: and their father gave them inheritance among their brethren.
>
> After this lived Job an hundred and forty years, and saw his sons, and his sons' sons, even four generations.
>
> So Job died, being old and full of days. (Job 42:10–17.)

Happy endings in classic novels or good movies sometimes enable us to escape our own suffering temporarily and make us feel good for the moment. Yet these fictional endings do not impact our own circumstances or permanently relieve our heartaches. The scriptural account of Job, however, serves as a divine type and witness of the Lord's promise that blessings will follow faithful endurance of adversity. In our own day, the Lord has promised that tribulations can be turned into triumphs and blessings can flow from the "water of affliction."

For verily I say unto you, blessed is he that keepeth my commandments, whether in life or in death; and he that is faithful in tribulation, the reward of the same is greater in the kingdom of heaven.

Ye cannot behold with your natural eyes, for the present time, the design of your God concerning those things which shall come hereafter, and the glory which shall follow after much tribulation.

For after much tribulation come the blessings. . . .

Remember this, which I tell you before, that you may lay it to heart, and receive that which is to follow. (D&C 58:2-5.)

Like Job, we are promised that adversity and affliction will yield glory and blessings. Thus we can come to understand and experience more fully the familiar saying, "The darkest hour is just before dawn." Suffering and sorrows not only can produce deferred blessings and glory but also may of themselves be blessings in disguise. Of this President Lorenzo Snow testified: "They [the Saints] may be afflicted and pass through numerous trials of a severe character, but these will prove blessings in disguise and bring them out brighter and better than they were before. The people of God are precious in His sight; His love for them will always endure, and in His might and strength and affection, they will triumph and be brought off more than conqueror." (*Teachings of Lorenzo Snow,* p. 121.)

Faithful endurance of adversity brings "riches" in mortality. Our souls are enlarged, our character is refined, our service is sanctified, and our enjoyment and appreciation of life are enriched. In addition to all of these adversity-induced blessings, there await greater rewards—even the "riches of eternity" that surpass all hopeful expectation. It is as the Lord has promised, "After much tribulation come the blessings"—both *here* and *hereafter.*

Earthly Rewards for Faithful Endurance

"After the trials there cometh the blessing," President George Q. Cannon testified. "We have never yet passed through severe afflictions without there being compensation in the shape of great blessings bestowed upon us. And so it will be. Trial will follow trial; but blessings will follow trial also." (*Gospel Truth*, p. 304.) The Lord has assured us that blessings await those who faithfully and patiently endure life's many hardships and heartaches. Very often, however, the promised blessings are not what we expect. They are, nonetheless, blessings and serve as evidence of the Father's love for his children. Inevitably these blessings are not only different from what we expected but also infinitely better because they are perfectly suited for our higher needs—needs we may not even have recognized before. This concept may be illustrated by the following true examples.

A successful businessman, at the pinnacle of his professional career, was diagnosed as having an extremely rare and debilitating medical condition. Naturally he asked, "Why me? Why this? Why at this time in my life?" Because of his medical condition he was forced to retire early from his prospering business. Years later he was able to recognize that his illness, though painful and difficult, was a blessing, not a trial. When he was healthy his business pursuits too often caused him to be away from his family. It was not uncommon for him to be out of town or in meetings during milestones, such as graduations, music recitals, and other special events, in the lives of his children. As a result he observed that his children were becoming emotionally distant from him and were straying spiritually from the strait and narrow path. Though his illness seemed such a trying burden at the time, it actually became a saving blessing in that it allowed him to be with his children more often—to teach them, to love and nurture them, and to provide spiritual guidance that he had previously neglected to give. After each of his sons faithfully served missions and married in the temple, almost as if the veil were temporarily lifted, he could see that his "adversity" had yielded spiritual rewards perhaps unobtainable otherwise.

When their lives seemed to be crumbling all around them, another family experienced unanticipated blessings in the form of enhanced family relationships. During a short span of time a son was seriously injured in the mission field, a grandfather died after a lingering illness, the mother underwent major surgery, the family finances became tenuous, and a rebellious teenager brought disharmony and emotional strife into the home. Just when they felt that they could not bear up under any more affliction, the father was diagnosed as having cancer. During the difficult days of recovering from surgery and the effects of chemotherapy, important blessings became readily apparent, though from unexpected sources. The family grew closer together than ever before, the rebellious teenager turned from his waywardness and came back to his parents with greater love and appreciation, and the parents' marriage was strengthened with a spirit of sweetness and consideration that had previously been lacking. From the darkest dilemmas of their lives came some of life's best and brightest blessings.

As seen in the previous examples adversity that may be perceived at first as being negative may be in fact positive; it may be family-saving, marriage-saving, or even life-saving and soul-saving. Blessings, in the guise of trials and troubles, can come to us in other ways as well. Development of character traits and individual strengths that facilitate significant service to others, greater peace and fulfillment in life, and deeper personal spirituality is also a blessing that comes "after much tribulation." The Apostle

Paul, who was personally and painfully acquainted with adversity, recognized this blessing. As a result of his deeper understanding of the role of adversity he did not shun suffering, nor did he contend against God; rather, he did "glory in tribulations." He wrote:

> Therefore being justified by faith, we have peace with God through our Lord Jesus Christ:
> By whom also we have access by faith into this grace wherein we stand, and rejoice in hope of the glory of God.
> And not only so, but we glory in tribulations also: knowing that tribulation worketh patience;
> And patience, experience; and experience, hope:
> And hope maketh not ashamed; because the love of God is shed abroad in our hearts by the Holy Ghost which is given unto us. (Romans 5:1–5.)

While we should not foolishly and unnecessarily seek out adversity as a means of acquiring blessings, we should try to recognize the blessings of growth and character enrichment that stem from faithful endurance. Patience, experience, hope, and many other beneficial traits and consequences can result from affliction. In this way weaknesses, afflictions, oppositions, and sufferings become strengths. "My strength is made perfect in weakness," declared Paul. "Most gladly therefore will I rather glory in my infirmities, that the power of Christ may rest upon me. Therefore I take pleasure in infirmities, in reproaches, in necessities, in persecutions, in distresses for Christ's sake: for when I am weak, then am I strong." (2 Corinthians 12:9–10; see also Ether 12:27.) Elder John Taylor added his testimony of this beneficial value of tribulation and identified other blessings which flow from adversity:

> There are many things that seem to us trials and difficulties, that perplex, annoy, and harass our spirits; yet

these very things, as one justly observed, are blessings in disguise, so many helps to us to develop our weaknesses and infirmities, and lead us to put our trust in God, and rely upon Him to give us a knowledge of ourselves, of our neighbors, and of the work of God; they have a tendency to develop principles of worth to our minds, and thus they serve as schoolmasters, helps, and instructors, and are to us as many blessings in disguise. In fact all things that we have to do with in the world, whether they are adversity or prosperity, whether they relate to ourselves or to others, if rightly appreciated and understood, may teach us a lesson that will be to our joy, probably not only in time, but in all eternity. We must know ourselves, learn what is in our nature—our weakness, our strength, our wisdom, our folly, and the like things that dwell in others, that we may learn to appreciate true and correct principles, and be governed by them whenever they are developed . . . that we may learn to look upon ourselves as eternal beings, acting in everything with a reference to eternity; that we may by and by secure to ourselves eternal exaltations, thrones, principalities, and powers in the eternal worlds. (In *Journal of Discourses* 1:366.)

Elder Lorenzo Snow also taught that faith is perfected and saving knowledge secured through trials and tribulation: "Many of you may have severe trials, that your faith may become more perfect, your confidence be increased, and your knowledge of the powers of heaven be augmented, and this before your redemption takes place" (*Teachings of Lorenzo Snow,* p. 121). These blessings acquired through adversity can benefit us throughout mortality and can prepare us for the inheritance of eternal glory. During the time he was President of the Church, Lorenzo Snow taught:

It is profitable to live long upon the earth and to gain the experience and knowledge incident thereto; for the Lord has told us that whatever intelligence we attain to in this life will rise with us in the resurrection, and the more knowledge and intelligence a person gains in this life the greater advantage he will have in the world to come. Some things we have to learn by that which we suffer, and knowledge secured in that way, though the process may be painful, will be of great value to us in the other life. (*Teachings of Lorenzo Snow,* p. 30.)

Acquisition of spiritual knowledge, perfection of faith, development of character, increasing of personal strengths, and strengthening of family relationships are all significant blessings derived from enduring well. As important as each of these is, there is another blessing resulting from adversity that perhaps transcends all other earthly rewards — the love of Christ. "Who shall separate us from the love of Christ?" asked the Apostle Paul. "Shall tribulation, or distress, or persecution, or famine, or nakedness, or peril, or sword? . . . Nay, in all these things we are more than conquerors through him that loved us. For I am persuaded, that neither death, nor life, nor angels, nor principalities, nor powers, nor things present, nor things to come, nor height, nor depth, nor any other creature, shall be able to separate us from the love of God, which is in Christ Jesus our Lord." (Romans 8:35–39.)

Neither suffering nor death, nor any manner of affliction, need interfere with or destroy the love of God in our lives. In fact one of the greatest blessings that may come to us through adversity is an increased awareness of the Savior's love; during such times of affliction, that pure love may be more profoundly felt in our lives than ever before. "My God hath been my support," Nephi wrote concerning the blessings of his own adversities. "He hath led me through mine afflictions in the wilderness; and he hath preserved me upon the waters of the great deep. He hath filled me with his love, even unto the consuming of my flesh." (2 Nephi 4:20–21.)

It is not uncommon to hear people who have experienced all manner of affliction and have known the depth and breadth of human suffering testify, with deep appreciation, of this blessing. One such woman taught me and touched me with her example. She bore a moving testimony of the pure love of Christ that had filled her life after her husband unexpectedly died of a heart attack. Despite the emotional shock and pain and the feelings of uncertainty and loneliness, she experienced a love *for* the Savior and a love *from* the Savior, the depths of which she had never before known. With gratitude she spoke of the opportunities and blessings—especially the abundant outpouring of the love of Christ—that her adversity had afforded her rather than of the sorrow and suffering that resulted.

Another family we knew and loved testified of this principle through the eloquence of their example. The young father was diagnosed as having terminal cancer and died not many months later. His wife had given birth to their third child shortly before his death. That the Lord would allow a young wife to be widowed and small children to be orphaned and denied the privilege of knowing and growing up with their father seemed, to all who knew them, such a terrible tragedy. Those of us who observed saw this adversity as unfair and unbearable, but those who actually suffered through it perceived it as a blessing, not a burden. They spoke of the increased love that came into their home and of the closeness they felt not only to each other but also to the Lord. While we on the outside felt so bad, they, like Paul, "gloried" in their tribulation. Through the outpouring of the love of Christ, what must have seemed to some as the worst of times became, in fact, one of the most blessed of times. The Lord has promised, "After much tribulation come the blessings." While some of the blessings of adversity must wait until later, the love of Christ and the strength and development of character such adversity can produce in us need not be deferred. Elder Marion G. Romney affirmed these principles with his personal testimony and pronounced an apostolic blessing upon those burdened with trials:

> My desire is to comfort and encourage and inspire all you faithful, humble people who are enduring, with patience and loneliness, pain, sorrow, and at times almost despair; you who languish in hospitals and nursing homes, and all you other shut-ins; you who mourn the loss of loved ones by death or transgression; you who are experiencing diminution of strength in mind and body. In sympathy and love I say to you and all the rest of us who are being tried in the crucible of adversity and affliction: Take courage; revive your spirits and strengthen your faith. . . .
>
> If we can bear our afflictions with the understanding, faith, and courage . . . we shall be strengthened and comforted in many ways. . . .
>
> Not only have I been impressed by the testimonies of others; I have been eyewitness to the operation of these principles in the lives of my own acquaintances. I have seen the remorse and despair in the lives of men who, in the hour of trial, have cursed God and died spiritually. And I have seen people rise to great heights from what seemed to be unbearable burdens.
>
> Finally, I have sought the Lord in my own extremities and learned for myself that my soul has made its greatest growth as I have been driven to my knees by adversity and affliction.
>
> To these things I bear solemn witness in the name of Jesus Christ, our beloved Savior, and in his name I invoke a comforting and sustaining blessing upon each of you. ("The Crucible of Adversity and Affliction," pp. 67–69.)

Eternal Rewards for Faithful Endurance

In the story of Job his losses were restored to him while he yet lived. He regained his family, friends, and prosperity. Sometimes the losses sustained in the course of life's adversities cannot be restored to us in mortality, nor can all of our anguish and affliction be completely eliminated. We are promised, however, that if we are faithful we will be beneficiaries of a divine law of compensation—one that is infinitely more generous and just than any earthly remuneration. President Lorenzo Snow spoke of this divine compensation and of how faithful endurance of mortal suffering will ultimately lead to even greater rewards in heaven:

> I suppose I am talking to some who have had worry and trouble and heart burnings and persecution, and have at times been caused to think that they never expected to endure quite so much. But for everything you have suffered, for everything that has occurred to you which you thought an evil at that time, you will receive fourfold, and that suffering will have had a tendency to make you better and stronger and to feel that you have been blessed. When you look back over your experiences you will then see that you have advanced far ahead and have gone up several rounds of the ladder toward exaltation and glory. (*Teachings of Lorenzo Snow,* p. 117.)

It is through the atonement of Jesus Christ that ultimately all losses can be restored, all suffering can cease, and all inequities and injustices can be rectified. "Subject to our doing 'all we can do,' the Atonement compensates for the harmful consequences of all our acts of independence," wrote Bruce C. Hafen, "both the consequences we may suffer and the consequences other people suffer through our actions. . . . This compensation is available not only to redress the effects of sin but also to redress the effects of bitterness resulting from judgment-call choices and undeserved adversity.'' (*The Broken Heart,* p. 41.) Although there is some mortal compensation for suffering, complete compensation and perfect peace must be deferred until the next life. President Spencer W. Kimball taught:

> This life, this narrow sphere we call mortality, does not, within the short space of time we were allowed here, give to all of us perfect justice, perfect health, or perfect opportunities. Perfect justice, however, will come eventually through a divine plan, as will the perfection of all other conditions and blessings—to those who have lived to merit them.
>
> On the earth there are many apparent injustices, when man must judge man and when uncontrollable situations seem to bring undeserved disaster, but in the judgment of God there will be no injustice and no soul will receive any blessing, reward, or glory which he has not earned, and no soul will be punished through deprivation or otherwise for anything of which he was not guilty. (*Teachings of Spencer W. Kimball,* pp. 46–47.)

This principle of divine compensation is part of the reward which is ''greater in the kingdom of heaven'' and the ''glory which shall follow after much tribulation'' (D&C 58:2–3). But there is a promised reward greater than the mere restoration of losses. Just as Job was blessed more in the latter end than in the beginning, we too are promised greater blessings than finite minds can fully fathom. ''For our light affliction, which is but for a moment,'' Paul assures us, ''worketh for us a far more exceeding and eternal weight of glory'' (2 Corinthians 4:17). The Lord's promise to the Prophet Joseph Smith also applies to us and our adversities: ''My son, peace be unto thy soul; thine adversity and thine afflictions shall be but a small moment; and then, if thou endure it well, God shall exalt thee on high; thou shalt triumph over all thy foes" (D&C 12:7–8). Exaltation in the kingdom and presence of God is the promised blessing to those who are faithful to the gospel of Jesus Christ and who endure well life's trials and tribulations. Although we may not completely comprehend while in mortality what exaltation really means, through the scriptures the Lord parts the veil and gives us an inviting glance of this most desirable state. In our moments of distress and discouragement these scriptural words bring solace and hope, remind us of "the glory which shall follow," and almost plead with us to hold fast to the iron rod despite the tempests of life's turmoils and troubles.

> Wherefore, as it is written, they are gods, even the sons of God—
> Wherefore, all things are theirs, whether life or death, or things present, or things to come, all are theirs and they are Christ's, and Christ is God's.
> And they shall overcome all things. . . .
> These shall dwell in the presence of God and his Christ forever and ever.
> These are they whom he shall bring with him, when he shall come in the clouds of heaven to reign on the earth over his people.
> These are they who shall have part in the first resurrection.
> These are they who shall come forth in the resurrection of the just.
> These are they who are come unto Mount Zion, and unto the city of the living God, the heavenly place, the holiest of all.
> These are they who have come to an innumerable company of angels, to the general assembly and church of Enoch, and of the Firstborn.

These are they whose names are written in heaven, where God and Christ are the judge of all.

These are they who are just men made perfect through Jesus the mediator of the new covenant, who wrought out this perfect atonement through the shedding of his own blood.

These are they whose bodies are celestial, whose glory is that of the sun, even the glory of God, the highest of all, whose glory the sun of the firmament is written of as being typical. (D&C 76:58–70.)

[They] shall inherit thrones, kingdoms, principalities, and powers, dominions, all heights and depths . . . and they shall pass by the angels, and the gods, which are set there, to their exaltation and glory in all things, as hath been sealed upon their heads, which glory shall be a fulness and a continuation of the seeds forever and ever.

Then shall they be gods, because they have no end; therefore shall they be from everlasting to everlasting, because they continue; then shall they be above all, because all things are subject unto them. Then shall they be gods, because they have all power, and the angels are subject unto them. (D&C 132:19–20.)

I add my personal testimony of the truthfulness of the gospel of Jesus Christ and of the hope and healing it provides in times of adversity and affliction. I bear witness of the promised peace the Savior extends to all who will take his yoke upon them. Because he has descended below all human anguish and affliction and has borne our infirmities, he can lift us up and draw all men unto him. It is my prayer that through him each of us may endure well our own adversities and be exalted on high. May we so live, not only in our times of trouble but also in our periods of peace and prosperity, that we may be among those seen in vision by John the Revelator:

These are they which came out of great tribulation, and have washed their robes, and made them white in the blood of the Lamb.

Therefore are they before the throne of God, and serve him day and night in his temple: and he that sitteth on the throne shall dwell among them.

They shall hunger no more, neither thirst any more; neither shall the sun light on them, nor any heat.

For the Lamb which is in the midst of the throne shall feed them, and shall lead them unto living fountains of waters: and God shall wipe away all tears from their eyes. (Revelation 7:14–17.)

Works Cited

Adams, A. K., ed. *The Book of Humorous Quotations.* New York: Dodd, Mead, & Co., 1969.

Ashton, Marvin J. *Be of Good Cheer.* Salt Lake City: Deseret Book Co., 1987.

———. " 'If Thou Endure It Well.' " *Ensign* 14 (November 1984): 20–22.

Benson, Ezra Taft. *Our Obligation and Challenge.* Address delivered at Regional Representatives' seminar, 30 September 1977.

———. *The Teachings of Ezra Taft Benson.* Salt Lake City: Bookcraft, 1988.

Brewster, Hoyt W., Jr. "It's OK to Be Spiritual and Still Have Fun." *Church News,* 10 March 1985, p. 11.

Bromiley, G. W., ed. *The International Standard Bible Encyclopedia.* 4 vols. Grand Rapids, Mich.: Eerdmans Publishing Co., 1979–88.

Brown, Hugh B. *Eternal Quest.* Edited by Charles Manley Brown. Salt Lake City: Bookcraft, 1956.

Byron, Ellen, comp. " 'The Best Advice I Can Give You.' " *Redbook* 169 (August 1987): 68–71.

Cannon, George Q. *Gospel Truth.* Edited by Jerreld L. Newquist. 2 vols. 1957. Reprint (2 vols. in 1). Salt Lake City: Deseret Book Co., 1987.

Cook, Lyndon W. *The Revelations of the Prophet Joseph Smith.* Salt Lake City: Deseret Book Co., 1985.

Evans, Richard L. *Richard Evans' Quote Book.* Salt Lake City: Publishers Press, 1971.

Faust, James E. "The Refiner's Fire." *Ensign* 9 (May 1979): 53–59.

Frankl, Viktor E. *Man's Search for Meaning.* Rev. ed. New York: Simon & Schuster, Washington Square Press, 1984.

Goaslind, Jack H. "Happiness." *Ensign* 16 (May 1986): 52–54.

Groberg, John H. "There Is Always Hope." In *Hope,* pp. 46–67. Salt Lake City: Deseret Book Co., 1988.

Hafen, Bruce C. *The Broken Heart.* Salt Lake City: Deseret Book Co., 1989.

Holland, Jeffrey R. " 'He Loved Them unto the End.' " *Ensign* 19 (May 1989): 25–26.

Holland, Jeffrey R., and Patricia T. Holland. *On Earth as it is in Heaven.* Salt Lake City: Deseret Book Co., 1989.

Hunter, Howard W. " 'Master, the Tempest Is Raging.' " *Ensign* 14 (November 1984): 33–35.

Kimball, Edward L., and Andrew E. Kimball Jr. *Spencer W. Kimball.* Salt Lake City: Bookcraft, 1977.

Kimball, Spencer W. *Faith Precedes the Miracle.* Salt Lake City: Deseret Book Co., 1972.

———. "The Lord Expects His Saints to Follow the Commandments." *Ensign* 7 (May 1977): 4–7.

————. "Small Acts of Service." *Ensign* 4 (December 1974): 2-7.

————. *The Teachings of Spencer W. Kimball.* Edited by Edward L. Kimball. Salt Lake City: Bookcraft, 1982.

Kushner, Harold S. *When All You've Ever Wanted Isn't Enough.* New York: Simon & Schuster, Pocket Books, 1986.

————. *When Bad Things Happen to Good People.* New York: Avon Books, 1981.

Larsen, Dean L. *Free to Act.* Salt Lake City: Bookcraft, 1989.

————. "The Peaceable Things of the Kingdom." In *Brigham Young University 1984-85 Devotional and Fireside Speeches,* pp. 71-76. Provo: University Publications, 1985.

Lewis, C. S. *A Grief Observed.* New York: Bantam Books, 1961.

————. *Mere Christianity.* New York: Macmillan, 1952.

————. *The Problem of Pain.* New York: Macmillan, 1962.

Livingood, Jay. "Quake's Heavy Hand Didn't Crush Testimony." *Church News,* 23 April 1977, p. 5.

McKay, David O. "Man's Free Agency—an Eternal Principle of Progress." *Improvement Era* 68 (December 1965): 1072-73, 1096-97.

Maxwell, Neal A. *All These Things Shall Give Thee Experience.* Salt Lake City: Deseret Book Co., 1979.

————. *But a Few Days.* Address delivered to religious educators. Salt Lake City: The Church of Jesus Christ of Latter-day Saints, 1983.

————. " 'Endure It Well.' " *Ensign* 20 (May 1990): 33-35.

————. "Irony: The Crust on the Bread of Adversity." *Ensign* 19 (May 1989): 62-64.

————. "Patience." In *1979 Devotional Speeches of the*

Year, pp. 215–20. Provo: Brigham Young University Press, 1980.

———. " 'Willing to Submit.' " *Ensign* 15 (May 1985): 70–73.

———. *A Wonderful Flood of Light.* Salt Lake City: Bookcraft, 1990.

———. " 'Yet Thou Art There.' " *Ensign* 17 (November 1987): 30–33.

Oaks, Dallin H. "Free Agency and Freedom." In *The Book of Mormon: Second Nephi, the Doctrinal Structure,* edited by Monte S. Nyman and Charles D. Tate Jr., pp. 1–17. Provo: Religious Studies Center, Brigham Young University, 1989.

Packer, Boyd K. "The Choice." *Ensign* 10 (November 1980): 20–22.

———. *The Holy Temple.* Salt Lake City: Bookcraft, 1980.

———. *"Let Not Your Heart Be Troubled . . ."* Brigham Young University Speeches of the Year. Provo, 4 October 1966.

———. *Teach Ye Diligently.* Salt Lake City: Deseret Book Co., 1975.

Peck, M. Scott. *The Road Less Traveled.* New York: Simon & Schuster, Touchstone Books, 1978.

Peterson, H. Burke. "Adversity and Prayer." In *Prayer,* pp. 105–9. Salt Lake City: Deseret Book Co., 1977.

Romney, Marion G. "The Crucible of Adversity and Affliction." *Improvement Era* 72 (December 1969): 66–69.

Smith, Joseph. *Teachings of the Prophet Joseph Smith.* Selected by Joseph Fielding Smith. Salt Lake City: Deseret Book Co., 1938.

Smith, Joseph F. *Gospel Doctrine.* Salt Lake City: Deseret Book Co., 1939.

———. "The Lesson in Natural Calamities." *Improvement Era* 9 (June 1906): 651–54.

Smith, Joseph Fielding. *Doctrines of Salvation*. Compiled by Bruce R. McConkie. 3 vols. Salt Lake City: Book- craft, 1954–56.

Smith, Lucy Mack. *History of Joseph Smith by His Mother*. Edited by Preston Nibley. Salt Lake City: Bookcraft, 1958.

Snow, Lorenzo. *The Teachings of Lorenzo Snow*. Com- piled by Clyde J. Williams. Salt Lake City: Book- craft, 1984.

Talmage, James E. "The Parable of the Unwise Bee." *Im- provement Era* 17 (September 1914): 1008–9.

Whitney, Orson F. *Life of Heber C. Kimball*. 1888. Re- print. Salt Lake City: Bookcraft, 1967.

Index

About the Author

Brent L. Top was born and raised in Idaho Falls, Idaho. He graduated with honors from Brigham Young University, receiving a bachelor's degree in history. From that institution he later received a master's degree in instructional media and ancient scripture and a Ph.D. in instructional science and technology.

The author served for many years in the Church Educational System as a seminary and institute instructor and administrator, later becoming an associate professor of Church History and Doctrine at Brigham Young University. He is currently associate dean of Religious Education at BYU. A popular teacher and speaker, he lectures with the Know Your Religion and Education Week series. He is the author or coauthor of several books, including *The Life Before; Forgiveness; Doctrinal Commentary on the Book of Mormon, Volume Four; Following the Living Prophets; Beyond Death's Door; An Inward Stillness;* and *Lord, I Would Follow Thee.* In addition, he has published numerous articles on religious, educational, historical, and sociological subjects.

The author is married to Wendy Cope Top, with whom he coauthored *Beyond Death's Door* and *An Inward Stillness.* They are the parents of four children and reside in Pleasant Grove, Utah.